JEAN COCTEAU

Born in 1889, Cocteau published his first collection of poems at the age of twenty and went on to produce work in a wide variety of other genres: paintings, drawings, set designs, novels, libretti, essays, choreography and autobiography, as well as plays and films. His early associates and collaborators included Diaghilev, Stravinsky and Nijinsky; Picasso, Satie and Massine, with whom he created *Parade*; Milhaud and Dufy – *Le boeuf sur le toit*; and Artaud, Honegger and Picasso again – *Antigone*. His musical mime play *Les mariés de la Tour Eiffel* was premiered in 1921 and was followed by many others, including *Orphée* (1926), *La voix humaine* (1929), *La machine infernale* (1934), *Oedipe-Roi* (1937, with Jean Marais) and *Les parents terribles* (1938). His films include *La belle et la bête*, *Les parents terribles*, *Orphée* and *Le testament d'Orphée*. He died in 1963.

JEREMY SAMS

Starting out as a piano accompanist, Sams has since worked extensively as a musical director, composer, translator and director for theatre, opera and television. His translations include Anouilh's *The Rehearsal* and *Becket* in the West End, Molière's *The Miser* and Cocteau's *Les Parents Terribles* for the Royal National Theatre, *La Cendrillon* for Welsh National Opera and *Figaro's Wedding* and *The Magic Flute* for English National Opera. He has directed plays for Greenwich Theatre, the Nottingham Playhouse and the West Yorkshire Playhouse, and composed scores for *The Wind in the Willows* and *Arcadia* at the Royal National Theatre and for *Talking Heads* and *The Importance of Being Earnest* in the West End.

A Selection of Other Volumes in this Series

*Published by Theatre Communications Group, distributed by Nick Hern Books

JEAN COCTEAU

LES PARENTS TERRIBLES (INDISCRETIONS)

Translated by Jeremy Sams

Introduced by Simon Callow

ROYAL NATIONAL THEATRE
London

NICK HERN BOOKS
London

A Nick Hern Book

Les Parents Terribles first published in this edition in
Great Britain in 1994 as a paperback original jointly by the
Royal National Theatre, London, and Nick Hern Books Ltd,
14 Larden Road, London W3 7ST

Reprinted 1995

Les Parents Terribles © Gallimard 1938
Translation © Jeremy Sams 1994

Jeremy Sams has asserted his moral right to be identified as
the translator of this work

Introduction copyright © Simon Callow 1994

Front cover: *La Lettre d'Amour* by Jean Cocteau, *c.* 1950,
Collection Severin Wunderman Foundation, Irvine, California

Typeset by Country Setting, Woodchurch, Kent TN26 3TB
Printed and bound by Cox & Wyman Ltd, Reading, Berkshire

ISBN 1 85459 256 4

Introduction

by Simon Callow

Cocteau's life was the longest photocall of all time. Prancing, strutting, preening, posing as the shutters clicked and the bulbs popped, for over fifty years Jean Cocteau was never far from the centre of the public scene, yet somehow always at an angle to it, in it, but not of it. Sometimes a gate-crasher, at other times the stage-manager, now critic and now reporter, he is present but elsewhere, his eyes glaze vatically (or is it just the opium?) as he turns his face to the camera to participate in the sacred rite of photography. What was merely a paparazzo's snap becomes a mythic image.

These images are oddly penetrating while being hauntingly contradictory; and the same is true of his work in general, that catalogue exhausting merely to list: aphorisms, ballet, comedy, design, erotica, film, glass work – one can go twice round the alphabet and still not run out. Staggering and staggeringly diverse, his unceasing productivity suggests another paradox: that of the driven dilettante, the industrious butterfly. Every casual effect was the result of extraordinarily hard work, every pose calculated and perfected. And yet the overall impression is of spontaneity, of – in the highest sense – amateurism. His work is suffused with love: of language, of form, of love itself. 'Instead of adopting Rimbaud's gospel, The time of the assassins has come,' he wrote in his erotic novel *Le Livre Blanc*, 'young people would do better to remember the phrase Love must be reinvented. The world accepts dangerous experiments in the realm of art because it does not take art seriously; but it condemns them in life.'

Cocteau's life is everywhere in his work, which is essentially a form of extended autobiography, and yet the man, omnipresent though he made himself, is strangely elusive. The Emperor Hadrian's self-observation – that all his public life contained something private, and all his private life something public – is equally true of Cocteau. Where the one begins and the other ends is almost impossible to say. His childhood, to which he constantly referred in his work and in his utterances, provided him with the themes that he continued to work out till the day he died: his awed love of the theatre ('the red-and-gold sickness' as he described it), its womb-like mysteries inevitably caught up with memories of his mother as she set off to see a play ('her red velvet dress, her necklace like the chandeliers in the boxes, her plume like a spotlight'); his complex relationship to the cruel beauty of his schoolfriend Dargelos whose savage treatment of him, both desired and feared, haunted his work to the end; and his poignant sense of innocence lost. Of all of these he made powerful myths.

His actual childhood, however, is something of a mystery, poorly documented and available to us only filtered through Cocteau's own mythomanic imagination. He was born in 1889 in a prosperous suburb of Paris (its Ascot: site of the fashionable racing track) to a family somewhat less prosperous than most of the neighbours. When he was nine, Cocteau's father shot himself for reasons which Cocteau never cared to explain beyond commenting that 'he would not have had to shoot himself for the same thing nowadays.' Was there a scandal, and if so was it sexual or financial? Was Cocteau himself involved? Nobody knows.

After the catastrophe, Cocteau and his sensible, elegant mother, already close, naturally grew closer and closer, until, at the age of fifteen, seeking to escape the emotional claustrophobia, he ran away from home, to Marseilles. There he lived, he claimed, for an entire year in the red-light district, gaining his sexual initiation with both sexes. This rite of passage completed, he returned home, an adult, continuing to live with his mother for many years. The great Oedipal themes – the absent father, perhaps destroyed by the son – and the overwhelming relationship with the mother infiltrate his work at every level, in innumerable variations, as they did his life. The most obvious pattern is the search for a son – a biological son, in two interesting cases in which Cocteau had proposed marriage; both women, no doubt wisely, rejected his proposal, the first having, to his bitter chagrin, aborted their child. For the rest, until the end of his life, he was rarely without a younger male companion: sons and lovers. All strikingly handsome, all were to a greater or lesser degree artistically gifted. Often Cocteau was the first person to recognise these gifts: he made it his business to identify, develop and promote their talents. Nurturing, facilitating, idealising them, he displayed almost maternal tenderness towards his son/lovers, helping them both psychologically and practically. Raymond Radiguet, Jean Desbordes, Marcel Khill, Jean Marais, and the last of them, Edouard Dermit; all owe their fulfilment to him. He saw in them what no one else had seen; he allowed them to become themselves. Interestingly, most of them were bisexual and some subsequently had children: the grand-children of Cocteau.

Les Parents Terribles was Cocteau's highly practical present to Jean Marais, the breathtaking beauty for whom the only possible phrase at that time of his life is god-like; certainly the only phrase that Cocteau could find. 'An Antinous sprung from the people,' he wrote of him, 'possessing all the characteristics of those hyperboreans mentioned in Greek mythology.' Cocteau met him, an untrained working-class lad with a troubled and unproductive childhood only just behind him, at auditions for a student

production of his unperformed play *Oedipe-Roi*. Immediately
Cocteau wanted to cast him in the title role, but was reluctantly
persuaded that this would upset the older and more experienced
members of the company; instead he cast him as Chorus, dressing
him in nothing but bandages. The sensation that this caused taught
the shrewd Marais that his uncommonly fine, and quite unworked-
on, physique was something that he had to strive against, which
meant resisting to some extent his new admirer's touching pride
in displaying it. Cocteau quickly grasped the point, too; he was
always willing to learn from his protégés, each of whom had in
different ways changed his life.

Cocteau's next play was the Arthurian romance *The Knights of the
Round Table*. Unsurprisingly, he cast Marais as Galahad, and
although Cocteau was unable to resist having him tear off his tunic
at a crucial point to reveal his bare torso, the role was a serious
acting challenge, one which Marais felt he had not brought off.
The next year, Cocteau wrote a role specifically for him, based
squarely on Marais' own personality. This is a young actor's
dream: the role he could play better than anyone else alive –
himself. It was not simply the role, however, that belonged to
Marais: to some extent the play itself was drawn from his life.

Les Parents Terribles chronicles the attempts of a young man to
escape the dominance of his mother, away from the magnetic pull
of her womb-like world, half-lit, alluring, disordered, into the cool
clean air of his girl-friend's sensible, organised life. Marais'
relationship with his mother (whom he called Rosalie after a
character in a play, just as Mik in *Les Parents Terribles* calls his
mother Sophie after the Princesse of Cleves) was not dissimilar;
nor, of course, was Cocteau's relationship with his. To that extent,
the role is a double portrait; a charming romantic gesture from
Cocteau to Marais.

The layers of allusion in the play hardly stop there, however: the
central device of the plot hinges on a father/son rivalry which is
drawn from Raymond Radiguet's life; the opening of Cocteau's
play alludes frankly, almost as an *hommage*, to a play of Jean
Desbordes, yet another lover. The names of the characters are
knowingly chosen: Yvonne is the name of the mother in the play,
but also that of the actress for whom the part was written, Yvonne
de Bray; Madeleine, the girl-friend's name, was the name of
Cocteau's first girl-friend, with whom he used to consort in his
little bachelor pad, just like the one in which Mik consorts with
his Madeleine in *Les Parents Terribles*. Finally, Georges, the
oddly absent and then all-too present father, was the name of
Cocteau's own father. In the words of Milorad in his perceptive
essay on the play, we have here 'a Pirandellian game between the
theatre and life.'

All this suggests the highly personal nature of the play, more personal even than Cocteau's many other *oeuvres à clef*. It amounts to a highly complex projection of many strands of his inner and outer lives; it is also a departure in his work which is at the same time a return. His theatre work had experimented and improvised endlessly with form: the surreal, dream-like *Orphée*, the speeded-up horror of his version of Sophocles' *Oedipus Rex,* the four radically different acts of his own version of the Oedipus story, *La Machine Infernale*, in which Jocasta passes from the boulevard of act one, to the dream play of act two, to the emotional intensities of act three, culminating with the stark, stripped-down force of the last. His *Knight of the Round Table* contained another daring innovation: a character who doesn't appear, but possesses other characters in turn.

His startling innovation in *Les Parents Terribles* was to play it absolutely straight. 'This time,' he wrote in the programme of the original production, 'I'm transporting you neither by Greek chariot, nor by aeroplane on the shoulders of Merlin nor in a little racing car, as in *Orphée*. Here instead is the Rolls-Royce of families, uncomfortable and ruinous . . . with this play, I'm resuming the tradition of boulevard theatre.' His aim, he claimed, was to rediscover the 'purple thread' of the theatre 'lost among the excesses of *staging*.' He added: 'I'm not blaming anyone: no one is more responsible for the excess than me.' His request on the title page of the play was a simple one: 'the set must be so solidly constructed that the doors can be constantly slammed.' He wanted to reach 'the large public . . . that mysterious mass;' he wanted to unite Marais and that public, but also he had a personal passion to evoke again the theatre of his youth. After all, the all-powerful plot of boulevard plays is not so very different from the gods' game when they trap Oedipus in the infernal machine of his destiny. 'This is where fate's just having fun with us,' says Leo in *Les Parents Terribles*. She means the plot, of course. Michael and Leo and Georges and Yvonne in *Les Parents Terribles* are trapped inexorably in the workings of the play's action, and the outcome is equally absurd and tragic.

Cocteau succeeded in all his ambitions: the play is a brilliant exercise in the manner of the *fin-de-siècle* boulevard; the commentary on human affairs that it offers is acute and terrible; and Marais had an enormous personal triumph, the audience recalling him to receive his standing ovation, Cocteau delightedly recorded, though he had returned to his dressing room and started to remove his costume. There was a lucrative run, terminated by the Conseil de Paris, which owned the theatre, denouncing the play for what it claimed to be its depiction of incestuous relationships; this of course only increased the play's appeal, and it ran on to capacity houses for another six months at another theatre.

Marais remained a central figure in Cocteau's life and work, though they both drifted off to other relationships. Cocteau continued to write boulevard theatre (including a one-act play for Edith Piaf) as well as more ambitious pieces on loftier themes (*Bacchus*, then *Renaud and Armide*, in rhyming couplets). His creative future lay more significantly in film, where, most often in collaboration with Marais, he created two or three of the most fascinating works of the French cinema. Although the period of his greatest artistic intensity had passed, he continued ceaselessly productive to the end. Among his last works were two he worked on simultaneously: the designs for an altarpiece emblazoned with symbols of the esoteric Rosicrucian order of which he was rumoured to be Grand Master, and an adaptation of the sleazy late fifties musical *The World of Suzy Wong*. The paradoxes and the contradictions never ceased till the day of his death, 11 October 1963, the same day as his great friend Piaf. He couldn't have planned it better.

Jean Cocteau, 1889-1963: a Chronology

1889   July 5: Clément Eugène-Jean-Maurice Cocteau born at Maisons-Laffitte.

1899   Cocteau's father commits suicide. The family goes to live with Mme Cocteau's father.

1900-07 Begins to frequent circus, theatres and concerts. Fails *baccalaureat* examination three times and gives up studies.

1908   Actor Edouard de Max organises a reading at the Théâtre Femina of poetry by the 18-year-old Jean Cocteau. His first published work appears in the magazine *Je sais tout*.

1909   Cocteau publishes his first collection of poems, *La Lampe d'Aladin*, at his own expense and founds the magazine *Schéhérazade* with Maurice Rostand and François Bernard. Meets impresario Serge Diaghilev.

1910   Cocteau's poems *Le Prince frivole* published. Meets Igor Stravinsky.

1911   Executes posters and drawings for Diaghilev's *Le Spectre de la Rose*.

1912   Nijinsky creates *Le Dieu bleu*, a ballet Cocteau had written in collaboration with Reynaldo Hahn.

1913   Works with Stravinsky on his ballet *David*.

1914-16 Excused from military service, serves as a volunteer ambulance corps-man at Reims, then in the trenches on the Belgian front. Meets the aviator Roland Garros with whom he makes several flights and in whose memory he later publishes *Le Cap de Bonne-Espérance*. Frequents Montmartre and Montparnasse where he meets Picasso, Braque, Derain, Juan Gris, Modigliani, Apollinaire, Max Jacob, Blaise Cendrars, Erik Satie, Kisling, and later Morand and Breton.

1917   Premiere of the ballet *Parade* (which Cocteau has conceived, with Picasso as designer, Satie as composer, Diaghilev as producer, and Massine as choreographer) provokes noisy demonstrations by factions in the audience. The first 'metaphor of the everyday' in ballet.

1918   Publication of Cocteau's *Le Coq et l'Arlequin*, a celebration of modern music including American jazz, leads to a quarrel with Stravinsky.

1919   Publishes *Ode à Picasso* and *Le Potomak*. Meets and falls in love with the 16-year-old Raymond Radiguet and encourages him to write. ·

1920   Premiere of Cocteau's 'spectacle concert' *Le Boeuf sur le toit*, music hy Darius Milhaud and decor by Raoul Dufy. With Radiguet, founds the review *Le Coq*.

1921   Premieres of *Le Gendarme incompris*, a musical farce by Cocteau and Radiguet, and the mime drama *Les Mariés de la Tour Eiffel*.

1922   The premiere of Cocteau's adaptation of Sophocles' *Antigone*, with Antonin Artaud as Tiresias, scenery by Picasso and music by Honegger, is disrupted by a group of Surrealists.

1923   Gives a lecture at the College de France, entitled 'Order Considered as Anarchy'. Publishes *Le Grand Ecart, Plain-chant*, and *Thomas l'Imposteur*. Raymond Radiguet dies of typhoid, aged 20.

1924   Cocteau becomes addicted to opium. His adaptation of *Romeo and Juliet* is staged, with Cocteau as Mercutio. Writes the scenario for the Ballets Russes' *Le Train bleu*. Publishes a volume of his drawings.

1925   An exhibition of his drawings and manuscripts opens in Brussels. Undergoes treatment for his addiction. Publishes *Cri écrit, L'Ange Heurtebise, Le Mystère de Jean l'Oiseleur, Prière mutilée*.

1926   Premiere of his play *Orphée*. Publishes *Maison de Sante* and *Le Rappel à l'Ordre*. An exhibition is held of his *Poésie plastique*.

1927   Premiere of the oratorio *Oedipus Rex*, on which he has collaborated with Stravinsky. Publishes *Opéra*. His *Le Pauvre Matelot*, with music by Milhaud, is performed.

1928   Publishes *Oedipe-Roi* and *Roméo et Juliette*. Undergoes further treatment for his addiction.

1929   *Les Enfants terribles, Une Entrevue sur la critique* are published and *La Voix humaine*, his one-act play for a single character, first performed.

1930   First performance of *Cantate*. Shoots his first film, *Le Sang d'un poète*. *Opium* is published.

1934   Premiere of *La Machine infernale*.

1937   A production of the play *Oedipe-Roi* with Jean Marais (whom Cocteau has discovered at an audition) as Oedipus. Cocteau arranges the come-back of American bantam-weight champion of the world, Al Brown. Premiere of *Les Chevaliers de la table ronde*.

1938   14 November: premiere of *Les Parents terribles* at the Théâtre des Ambassadeurs. The play is accused of immorality and is closed on 23 December by the Municipal Council of Paris which owns the theatre. It re-opens the following year at the Théâtres des Bouffes-Parisiens.

1940   Premiere of *Les Monstres sacrés*. Edith Piaf performs the monologue Cocteau has written for her, *Le Bel Indifférent*. He undergoes his last treatment for opium addiction. *La Fin du Potomak* published.

1941   Premiere of *La Machine à écrire*, which is violently attacked by critics. Writes *Renaud et Armide* for Jean Marais. A revival of *Les Parents terribles* opens in October, is closed by the Prefect of Police, and re-opens at the end of December. Designs sets and costumes for Feydeau's *La Main Passe*. Writes dialogue for the film *Le Baron fantôme*, directed by Serge de Poligny, and appears himself as the baron.

1945   Begins filming *La Belle et la bête*, with Jean Marais as the Beast.

1946   The ballet of *Le Jeune Homme et la mort*. Premiere of *L'Aigle à deux tetes*.

1947   Meets Edouard Dermit, whom he will 'adopt' as his son. *La Difficulté d'être* published.

1948   Films *Les Parents terribles*.

1949   Cocteau is decorated as a Chevalier of the Legion d'Honneur. His adaptation of Tennessee Williams' *Streetcar Named Desire* opens. *Lettre aux Americains* published.

1950   His film *Orphée* wins the International Critics Prize at the Venice Film Festival.

1951   Begins to edit a personal diary, *Le Passé Defini*. The first volume is published in 1983. Contributes commentaries for several films.

1952   Publishes *Le Chiffre sept*, *Gide vivant*, *Le Journal d'un inconnu*.

1953   Ballet *La Dame à la licorne* opens at Munich.

1956-59   Receives an honorary doctorate at Oxford University.
Works on decorations for the chapel of Saint-Pierre at
Villefranche-sur-mer, for the marriage hall at the Hôtel
de Ville in Menton, and for the Chapel of Saint-Blaise-
des-Simples at Milly-la-Forêt; makes lithographs and
starts working in pottery; paints frescoes for the
exhibition *Earth and the Cosmos*. Cocteau, visiting
London in 1959 as a member of the chorus when
Stravinsky conducts *Oedipus Rex*, decorates the London
church Notre-Dame-de-France, Leicester Place, WC2.

1960   His film *Le Testament d'Orphée* shown in Paris.
(Director François Truffaut had contributed the prize
money he won for his film *The Four Hundred Blows*
towards the making of it.)

1961   Promoted to Commander of the Legion d'Honneur.

1962   An exhibition of Cocteau's work opens in Tokyo. Begins
work on the 'bastion' of Menton and the chapel of Notre-
Dame-de-Jerusalem at Fréjus. Records a 'Message for
the Year 2000'. Publishes *Cordon ombilical, Picasso
1919-61,* and *Requiem.*

1963   Writes an adaptation of *The World of Suzy Wong* with
Raymond Gérôme. Suffers a heart attack in Paris and
returns home to Milly-la-Forêt, where he is cared for by
Jean Marais and Edouard Dermit. On October 11, a few
hours after the death of Edith Piaf, Cocteau dies.

Reprinted by kind permission of the Royal National Theatre

LES PARENTS TERRIBLES

Characters

YVONNE

LEO

MADELEINE

GEORGE

MICHAEL

Les Parents Terribles was first performed in this translation in Britain on the Lyttelton stage of the Royal National Theatre on 21 April 1994. Press night was 5 May. The cast was as follows:

GEORGE	Alan Howard
LEONIE (LEO)	Frances de la Tour
YVONNE	Sheila Gish
MICHAEL	Jude Law
MADELEINE	Lynsey Baxter

Musicians David Berry, Steven Buckley and Michael Haslam
Directed by Sean Mathias
Designed by Stephen Brimson Lewis
Lighting by Mark Henderson
Music by Jason Carr
Front cloth designed by Ricardo Cinalli Company
Voice Work Jeannette Nelson

ACT ONE

Scene One

YVONNE's *room. Considerable disorder. A bed, some chairs. Three doors off: to the bathroom, to the hall, and to* LEO's *room. As the curtain rises* GEORGE *runs from the bathroom to* LEO's *door, shouting, slamming doors* . . .

GEORGE. Leo! Leo! Quick, quick, come quickly . . . Where are you?

LEO (*off*). Has Michael turned up yet?

GEORGE. I think it's something to do with Michael . . . hurry up.

LEO (*opening her door, slipping on an elegant house coat*). What is? What's happened?

GEORGE. Yvonne's taken an overdose.

LEO (*incredulous*). What?

GEORGE. Her insulin . . . she must have overfilled the syringe.

YVONNE *is revealed in the doorway of the bathroom. She is wearing a towelling dressing-gown, scarcely able to stand, as pale as death.*

LEO. Yvonne . . . My God what have you done? (YVONNE *is unwilling to be helped.*) Speak to me. Say something.

YVONNE (*barely intelligible*). Sugar . . .

GEORGE. I'll phone the clinic . . .

LEO. Stay where you are, keep calm. Thank God I'm here.

GEORGE. Oh damn and blast, it's Sunday, there won't be a soul there . . .

LEO. You should know by now that you've got to eat something after your insulin, and if you don't eat you need sugar.

GEORGE. Oh God, yes, the sugar.

He goes into the bathroom and returns with a glass of water. LEO *takes it and tries to get* YVONNE *to drink.*

LEO. Come on make an effort. Don't go all floppy on me. You don't want to die do you; not without seeing Michael again?

YVONNE *sits up a bit and drinks.*

GEORGE. God, Leo, I'm such an ass. If it hadn't been for you she'd have died. I'd've just let her die . . . out of sheer stupidity.

LEO (*to* YVONNE). How are you feeling?

YVONNE. Better. It works straight away. Look, I'm terribly sorry, that was grotesque . . .

GEORGE. And the doctor told me so many times, 'Never use household sugar, there's all sorts of muck in it. Use cane sugar, then you know it's pure'. And we always keep the glass ready, with the sugar, with the pure sugar dissolved in it. Just in case. And I completely . . .

YVONNE. Don't be silly, it's my fault.

LEO. It absolutely is your fault. You've been behaving like a complete madwoman.

YVONNE (*smiling*). Well, perhaps I have been a tiny bit madder than usual.

GEORGE. You have, that's why I couldn't think straight.

YVONNE. Well, thank God Leo's still sane. That's something anyway, you know I wouldn't have let Michael find me like . . . that. I wouldn't have upset him for the world.

GEORGE. If only he were as considerate as you.

YVONNE (*sitting up a bit*). So thank you, Leo. I should tell you what happened. It was five o'clock, time for my jab, and I was thinking, good, that'll be something to do. And then I heard the lift so I rushed out to see if it was . . . To see who it was. Only it wasn't for us it was downstairs or somewhere. So I went back, into the bathroom and I suddenly felt awful . . . Because I'd forgotten my sugar, you see, and then by some miracle George came and found me.

GEORGE. It was a miracle. I just came to see if you were having a nap.

LEO. What's all this nonsense about miracles? You were just miles away as usual, beavering away, the man in the moon. Then you heard a clock strike five – so the moonman came down to earth and met his own wife in her own room. Which is hardly a miracle.

GEORGE. Well, alright then it was a happy coincidence.

YVONNE. No, it was a miracle, Georgy. If it weren't for you . . .

GEORGE. . . . . If it weren't for your sister . . .

YVONNE. If it weren't for *both* of you I would have turned a silly fuss about nothing into a complete nightmare.

GEORGE. I'm sorry Yvonne, but it's a bit more than a fuss about nothing. Michael didn't come home last night, he slept somewhere else. We haven't heard a peep out of him, he could be anywhere. He knows you, he knows full well what a state you get into . . .

YVONNE. I don't care as long as I know he's all right. But no-one's in on a Sunday so how can we know? D'you think something awful's happened, and his friends haven't dared phone us up and tell us?

GEORGE. If something awful'd happened we'd've found out straight away. One always does. No really I think this is outrageous behaviour. *Un*believable!

YVONNE. But where d'you think he's got to?

LEO. Look Yvonne, you've had a shock, don't get worked up. George, don't get her worked up. Go back to your study – we'll call you if we need you.

YVONNE. Yes darling, go back to work . . .

GEORGE (*exiting*). I'm just doing some sums. But I keep on losing my place and having to start again.

Scene Two

YVONNE. Leo, where's the boy been sleeping. Doesn't he know he's driving me mad..? Why hasn't he called me..? It's not hard just to make a phone call.

LEO. Well, sometimes it is – if you have to lie and you're not a very good liar and if you're as clumsy and as transparent as Michael is . . .

YVONNE. But why would Mickey lie to me?

LEO. Well, two possibilities. Either he's too embarrassed to call or to come back. *Or* he's having such a peachy time wherever he is that he wouldn't dream of doing either. So . . . he has to be hiding something.

YVONNE. There's not much you can teach me about my own son. There's no question of him forgetting to ring. If he hasn't rung, it's because he must somehow be in mortal danger.

LEO. Don't be melodramatic. You can always telephone someone. He just doesn't want to, that's all.

YVONNE. You've been behaving oddly ever since this morning. As if you *knew* something.

LEO. I don't know anything. But I'm sure of something – which is a different matter.

YVONNE. Sure of what?

LEO. It's not worth telling you – you wouldn't believe me. You'd just say, but that's *un*believable. The only *un*believable thing being that the whole family's been using that ridiculous turn of phrase lately.

YVONNE. But it's one of Mickey's phrases.

LEO. I wonder where it comes from. It's peculiar . . .

YVONNE (*laughing*). What's so peculiar? You know us. We probably stole it . . . which wouldn't be strange behaviour for a bunch of rogues, thieves, vagabonds and madmen, would it? Living in a gypsy camp as you're constantly reminding us . . .

LEO. Now don't be silly, just because I once called you the raggle-taggle gypsies, and said you lived in a gypsy encampment. Which you do. And that you're all as mad as a bag of snakes. Which you are. Madder.

YVONNE. All right, we live in a gypsy camp, and all right we're mad. But whose fault's that?

LEO. Oh God, you're not going to wheel out Grandpa again, are you?

YVONNE. Yes. Why not Grandpa? Grandpa who used to collect semicolons. Who counted all the semicolons in Balzac. You remember, 'You may be surprised to hear there are 37,000 semicolons in *La Cousine Bette*'. Except he was always worrying that he had lost count and he'd start all over again. But in those days you didn't say mad, you said eccentric. Nowadays, with a head start and a following wind, pretty much everybody's mad.

LEO. Let's call you lot eccentrics, then. Obsessives at least, you'll admit to that.

YVONNE. You're a bit of an obsessive yourself . . .

LEO. Well, possibly . . . I'm certainly obsessive about order, like you are about disorder. Which is why uncle left his tiny fortune to me. To keep you all on the straight and narrow.

YVONNE. Leonie!

LEO. Now don't be angry. I don't mind supporting you all. On the contrary. I admire George more than anybody. It's a privilege to help him continue with his research.

YVONNE. I'm sorry, but I've never understood you of all people taking George's researches remotely seriously. I mean talk about eccentric – he defines the term. The underwater sub-machine gun, indeed. I'mean, frankly, at his age, it's ludicrous . . .

LEO. All right, maybe George is just an overgrown schoolboy. All he's ever read is comic books and a surfeit of Jules Verne. And maybe he is a bit of a dilettante – but at heart he's a proper serious inventor. And you should at least give him credit for that.

YVONNE. That business with the war office. It's only because the minister was at school with Georgy. And it's not as if they've actually placed an order yet . . . and as for the gun, you know what I think, that's just what the raggle taggle gypsies need. Their latest sideshow, 'George and his Amazing Gun. Shoots real bullets underwater, roll up, roll up'. And since I do nothing all day but play patience in my dressing gown, I could be Gypsy Esmerelda, fortune teller. And you could be . . . of course, the strong lady. And Mickey.. Mickey would be . . .

LEO. The Eighth Wonder of the World.

YVONNE. Now that's not fair.

LEO. There are two distinct tribes in this world, children, and grown-ups. I, alas, fall into the latter category . . . you . . . George . . . and Michael . . . you belong to the former. Children who will always be children, and as children do, commit the most appalling crimes, apparently thoughtlessly..

YVONNE. Shut up. Listen. (*Silence.*) No . . . I thought I heard a car. Mickey will have drunk some champagne – that's it, and he's not used to it. So he'll have stayed with a friend. Perhaps he's still got a hangover, he'll be crippled with embarrassment, poor lamb.

LEO. You're completely blind.

YVONNE. What?

LEO (*slowly*). Yvonne, Michael has been spending the night with a woman.

YVONNE. Michael?

LEO. Yes Michael.

YVONNE. You're out of your mind. Mickey's just a child, you said so yourself a minute ago . . .

LEO. You don't listen. I said that you and George and Michael were children, and therefore dangerous – as opposed to other people who are grown-ups, and therefore less dangerous, that's all. But Michael isn't a child, not in the sense you mean. Not any more. He's a man. He's twenty-two.

YVONNE. Ah well!

LEO. You're fantastic! You sow the seeds, and you can't see what you're reaping.

YVONNE. What am I sowing? What am I reaping? What are you talking about?

LEO. You've sowed dust and dirty washing and old cigarette ends. And reaped . . . well, put it this way, Michael has been choking on the woodsmoke of your old gypsy camp and has had to get out to get some fresh air.

YVONNE. And you say he's gone to get some fresh air, what, with women? That he's seeing whores, is that it?

LEO. Now, there's a typical mother's reaction. You know why he hasn't called. So's not to hear 'Mickey darling, *do* come home, Papa wants a word' or some such nonsense. I'm the only one here, and – this is ridiculous – me, the tidy one, the obsessive one, I'm the only one who's not behaving like a dyed-in-the-wool bourgeois.

YVONNE. Pah!

LEO. All right, what's a bourgeois family . . . ?

YVONNE. Puh!

LEO. No I'm asking you. They're rich, orderly, with servants . . . and we're penniless, disorderly, and without servants. Or rather with no servants who've ever lasted more than four days. So I do all that (with the help of a daily, who won't do Sundays). But, even so, bourgeois to our grubby finger tips. The middle class gypsies. 'Cos, let's face it, we're not artists, we're not bohemians, not remotely. So there you have it.

YVONNE. I don't see what you're getting so steamed up about.

LEO. I'm not – I am very calm and very composed. It's just there are times when your gypsy camp gets too much to bear. Have you any idea why whole mountains of dirty washing pile up in Michael's room? Or why George might just as well do his sums in the dust on his desk-top? Or why the bath tub's been blocked for weeks now? Well, I'll tell you. It's because, just now and then, I get a kind of perverse delight in watching you getting stuck knee-deep in the quagmire of your own mess – but then my obsessive nature gets the better of me and I save you all from . . . I don't know what . . . collapse, chaos, cholera . . .

YVONNE. So you're saying our gypsy life has pushed Michael out. Forced him to find – something else . . . with a woman . . .

LEO. I am. And he's not the first.

YVONNE. You don't mean George?

LEO. On the contrary, I do mean George.

YVONNE. Are you saying George has been deceiving me?

LEO. Well, why not . . . you've been deceiving him!

YVONNE. Me . . . With whom? Since when?

LEO. With Michael, since the day he was born. On that day you ceased to have eyes for George and only had eyes for Michael. You were in love . . . and your love grew and grew and grew, just as he did. And George was left out. So it shouldn't surprise you that he sought affection elsewhere. That he occasionally decamped.

YVONNE. All right, suppose that any of this nonsense is true . . . and suppose George – who's never shown the remotest interest in anything other than his so-called inventions – has a mistress. And suppose Michael – who, excuse me, tells me *everything*, I'm his best friend, we're more like chums, – *did* spend the night with a woman, why haven't you told me 'til now?

LEO. Because I didn't think you were totally blind. I thought, no, Yvonne's putting a brave face on it, but she knows . . .

YVONNE (*she should find this difficult*). Well, as far as George is concerned . . . I can see why he might . . . well, you know. After twenty years a marriage changes shape. And after a while there's a sort of implicit understanding between husband and wife which makes certain things . . . certain overtures . . . very embarrassing . . . almost indecent . . . sometimes impossible.

LEO. You are a very strange woman, Yvonne.

YVONNE. Actually, I'm not . . . but I'm sure I seem strange to you, there's such a gulf between us. You've always been so beautiful, so *soignée*, elegant, brilliant – and I was born an utter mess, with snuffles and hay fever, my hair all over the place – faffing around like a wet hen in a high wind. And if I try and tart myself up I always look like . . . well, a tart.

LEO. You're forty-five for God's sake, and I'm forty-seven.

YVONNE. You've always looked younger than me.

LEO. Didn't stop George choosing you. He was engaged to me, and he chose you. Just like that . . .

YVONNE. You didn't seem to mind at the time. You practically pushed us together.

LEO. Well, that's my business. I respect George. I was afraid that

with me it was all here. (*Taps her head.*) With you it was all
there and there. (*She indicates her heart and between her legs.*)
Also I had no idea that you were so desperate to have a son –
and children like you invariably get what they want – *nor* that
you would be so besotted with your son that you'd ignore
George completely.

YVONNE. He could have found consolation with you.

LEO. You wanted me to sleep with George to take him off your
hands . . . Why would he want me? It's young flesh he's after.

YVONNE. Don't be absurd . . .

LEO. You don't believe me but I know I'm right. And there's a
ghost in this house. The ghost of a very young girl – and she's
everywhere . . .

YVONNE. No, come on, that's *un*believable.

LEO. Oh there's our new catch phrase again. It came in with
George. He had it before Michael. Michael caught it off him,
and you caught if off Michael. It's like the clap.

YVONNE. So you think Michael's deceiving me too . . . I mean,
lying to me?

LEO. No, you were right first time. He's been deceiving you. Is
deceiving you.

YVONNE. That's completely unthinkable. Completely impossible.
I'm sorry but I can't conceive of it. It can't be possible.

LEO. You see you don't mind George deceiving you. That's fine.
But with Michael, it's quite a different affair.

YVONNE. You're lying to me. Michael's always seen me as his
best friend. He tells me everything . . .

LEO. No mother is a friend to her son. He soon spots the spy
hiding behind the friend. And the jealous woman behind the
spy.

YVONNE. Mickey doesn't think of me as a woman.

LEO. No, that's where you're wrong. You don't think of him as a
man. He may still be a little boy to you but in Michael's eyes
you've become a woman. And your mistake is not being a
slightly more seductive one. He's looked at you, thought about
it, and made up his mind. He's flown the coop. He's decamped
too.

YVONNE. And where would Michael find enough time to pay
suitable homage to this mysterious temptress?

LEO. Time's elastic. With a bit of skill one can always give the impression of being somewhere, while in fact being somewhere else altogether.

YVONNE. Michael's working very hard.

LEO. Michael is not working very hard. Nor do you wish him to. In fact you wish him not to.

YVONNE. That's outrageous.

LEO. You've always prevented him from taking a job.

YVONNE. They were stupid jobs and would've meant him rubbing shoulders with, I don't know, movie people, the motor trade, awful people.

LEO. Did you encourage him to meet boys or girls of his own age? Did you ever talk about marriage?

YVONNE. What, his marriage?

LEO. Why not? Many young people get married at twenty-three, twenty-four . . .

YVONNE. Mickey's a baby.

LEO. What if he isn't anymore?

YVONNE. I'd be the first to find him a woman . . .

LEO. Yes, hand-picked. Some plain, gormless bit of fluff, who'd be no challenge to your supremacy.

YVONNE. That's not true. Michael's free. In as much as I can let him be free. He's a very special trusting boy. I wouldn't want to see him hurt.

LEO. I warn you, don't keep him under lock and key. He'll spot what you're up to – and hate you for it.

YVONNE. Oh, aren't we the psychologist all of a sudden. My God, there's someone at the door. (*We hear the bell.*) Go, Leo, go and see, quickly. I don't think I've got the strength.

LEO *exits.* YVONNE, *left alone, grabs the bag left by* LEO *on the bed, opens it, looks at the pocket mirror, powders her nose, pats her hair. She only just has time to throw the bag back on the bed before* GEORGE *and* LEO *enter.* GEORGE *turns on the light.*

Scene Three

YVONNE. Who turned the lights on?

GEORGE. I did. Sorry I'll turn them off . . . I just thought . . . It was so dark in here . . .

YVONNE. I like the darkness. Who was it?

LEO. Someone for the doctor upstairs, got the wrong floor. The Doctor's always out hunting on a Sunday.

Silence.

GEORGE. Any news?

YVONNE. No . . . the bell rang.

GEORGE. The specialist's off hunting too. You could bleed to death on a Sunday, no-one'd be any the wiser.

YVONNE. Anyway. I'm being stupid – he's got the spare keys.

GEORGE. I think it's disgraceful that the keys to this flat are knocking around any old where.

YVONNE. Who knows, he could have dropped them in the gutter somewhere.

GEORGE. And one day we'll wake up to find we've all been murdered in our beds. Then he'd be sorry. He'd better give them to me.

LEO. It's a pity I can't record your dialogue and play it back to you.

MICHAEL *enters while they're talking. He looks rather larky – like a boy who's just played a practical joke.*

YVONNE. What time is it?

MICHAEL. Six o'clock.

They all get up suddenly.

MICHAEL. It's not a ghost – it's only me.

GEORGE. Michael – you frightened your mother out of her wits. Look at her. How did you get home?

MICHAEL. By the front door. I took the stairs four at a time. Let me . . . get my breath back. Now Sophie bear, what's the matter?

GEORGE. You mother isn't at all well.

MICHAEL. Sophie – is it all my fault you're poorly?

Tries to kiss her. She rejects him.

YVONNE. Don't touch me.

MICHAEL. Well, all these long faces. You look as if I've committed some terrible crime.

GEORGE. You're not that far off, my boy. Your mother literally nearly died of worry.

MICHAEL. I'm sorry. I come back, *dying* to see you all, to see the gypsies again. To give Mama a kiss. And now I feel really awful . . .

GEORGE. And so you should. Where d'you think you've been?

MICHAEL. Let me get my breath back. I've so much to tell you all.

GEORGE. You didn't come back last night – you slept out – you didn't tell us when you'd be coming back.

MICHAEL. Look, Papa, I'm twenty-two . . . and it's the first time I've done it. Isn't it . . . ?

YVONNE. Where have you been? Your father asked you where you've been.

MICHAEL. Now, calm down children – Oh sorry, I mean, listen Papa, listen Aunt Leo – only don't spoil everything. What I wanted to say . . .

YVONNE. You wanted! *You* wanted! Really! Your *father* runs the household here. Anyway, he wants to speak to you. Go with him to his study.

LEO. Astonishing.

MICHAEL. No, Sophie, no. Firstly because Papa doesn't have a study, he has a dusty old box-room. And secondly, I want to talk to you, on your own, before I talk to anyone else.

GEORGE. My dear boy . . .

YVONNE. Perhaps if Michael finds it easier to talk to me you ought to leave us alone together.

LEO. Of course.

YVONNE. If Mickey's got something on his mind it's quite natural that he should want to tell his mother. George, you go back to work. Leo, you keep him company.

MICHAEL. Papa, Auntie, please don't be angry with me. I'll tell you everything, but all in good time. I'm bursting to tell you.

YVONNE. It's not serious, is it, Mickey?

MICHAEL. No. I mean yes.

YVONNE. George, you're unnerving the boy.

MICHAEL. Yes, you are, a bit.

LEO. Well good luck to you both.

GEORGE (*leaving*). I still want to talk to you, my boy. I'm not going to let you off that easily.

MICHAEL. Of course not.

GEORGE *closes the door.*

Scene Four

MICHAEL. Now Sophie. Gorgeous little Sophie. You're not angry with me are you? (*He gives her a puppyish hug.*)

YVONNE. Can't you kiss me without knocking me over..? Or messing up my hair..? Don't kiss me in my ear. I hate that Michael, *really*.

MICHAEL. Sorry. I didn't do it on purpose.

YVONNE. You are the giddy limit, really you are.

MICHAEL. But, Sophie – hello, what's this? You've got lipstick on.

YVONNE. I haven't.

MICHAEL. You jolly have. And powder. Excuse me, let's get to the bottom of this. Who's all this for, eh? Unbelievable. That's real ruby red deep gloss, kiss-me, kiss-me lipstick.

YVONNE. I was as pale as a corpse. I didn't want to frighten your father.

MICHAEL. No, don't wipe it off – it suits you.

YVONNE. Not that you ever look at me!

MICHAEL. Sophie – I do believe you're making a scene. And I don't need to be looking at you all the time, I know you by heart.

YVONNE. Exactly, you never look at me. You never even notice me.

MICHAEL. No, that's where you're wrong. I do notice you – out of the corner of my eye. And I notice that you're rather letting yourself go. Now, if you'd only allow me to do your hair and make you up . . .

YVONNE. Oh yes, fine goings on.

MICHAEL. Sophie, you're sulking. You're still angry with me.

YVONNE. I never sulk, and I'm not angry with you, Mickey. I'd just adore to know what the hell's going on.

MICHAEL. Have patience. All will be revealed.

YVONNE. Well?

MICHAEL. Please. Must you look so serious?

YVONNE. Mickey!

MICHAEL. Now you promise you won't go all loopy on me, no family behaviour, no gypsy camp hysteria? Just hear me out until I'm finished. All right? Promise?

YVONNE. I'm not promising anything in advance.

MICHAEL. You see!

YVONNE. People outside this house are obviously flattering you and humouring you. But I'm telling you things as they really are.

MICHAEL. All right, I'll go to Papa, he'll pretend to be finishing one of his endless sums and then go, 'Ah yes my boy, what seems to be the . . . er . . . '.

YVONNE. Don't make fun of your father. At least not of his work.

MICHAEL. But you're always making fun of the underwater thingummy whatsit.

YVONNE. That's different. It's bad enough that I let you call me Sophie.

MICHAEL. What!

YVONNE. I should have kept you on a tighter rein – I shouldn't have let your untidiness get to its present state . . . I mean have you seen your room, it's a pigsty . . . you'll allow me to finish . . . a pigsty . . . when I go in there I get positively *assaulted* by your dirty laundry.

MICHAEL. . . . . And you always said you *liked* seeing my things all higgledy-piggledy – you said you hated drawers and cupboards and mothballs and all that.

YVONNE. I never said anything of the sort.

MICHAEL. Excuse me!

YVONNE. Well, a century and a half ago I might have said that it was sweet seeing your boy's things scattered all over my room.

When you were little. But one day I noticed that your 'boy's things' had become men's things, men's vests and smelly socks and pants. Which is when I asked you to keep your things out of my room, which was looking more and more like a battlefield!

MICHAEL. Mama!

YVONNE. Aha! Not Sophie any more. You do remember there was a big fuss at the time.

MICHAEL. That's 'cos you stopped tucking me up in bed. We had a big big fight about that . . .

YVONNE. Mickey bear. I carried you up to bed until you were eleven, after which you got too heavy, so you hung round my neck, and you'd put your feet on my slippers, do you remember?, and we'd march up the wooden hill together. Then one evening you made fun of me tucking you in – and I thought, right my boy, you can go to bed on your own from now on.

MICHAEL. Sophie bear. Let me sit on your bed. Let me snuggle up to you, go on, right up to you. (*He does so.*) Now. No, I don't want you to look at me. Let's both look out into the night, at the house opposite.

YVONNE. You're preparing the ground far too carefully. I fear the worst.

MICHAEL. Now, you promised to be awfully, awfully sweet to me.

YVONNE. I promised you nothing of the sort.

They hold that pose, their faces lit by a light from the flat opposite.

YVONNE. Are you in debt?

MICHAEL. Sophie, shut up, don't be daft.

YVONNE. Michael . . .

MICHAEL. Just shut up.

YVONNE. Alright Mickey, I'm shutting up. I'm listening. Now speak.

MICHAEL (*quickly – embarrassed – his mother's face crumples and becomes appalled and appalling as he speaks*). Sophie. Look, I'm very very happy and wanted to be quite sure of my happiness before I shared it with you. Because if you're not happy as well, happy for me, then that would be awful. You understand? Now, let me tell you what's happened, at college I've met this young girl . . .

YVONNE. But there aren't any girls at your college.

MICHAEL. Look, hear me out will you? I haven't just been doing drawing – I took a shorthand typing course too; Papa said he might be able to get me a job as a secretary but I had to have typing. So I gave it a whirl – but you thought the job was a bad idea so I packed it in. I'd been, what, two, three times and then, miracle of miracles, I met a girl, a young woman really . . . well, she's three years older than me. Her friend, or guardian I suppose, was this old chap, fifty or so – widower – looked after her – treated her like his daughter, or rather he'd had a daughter who'd died so she reminded him of . . . Anyway, I saw her again, and again. I started skipping classes. And just doing drawing to bring home – you know, cauliflowers, busts of Homer . . . I wouldn't have told you about it if she hadn't decided to break free from this old chap, who was a bit soft on her I reckon, and start from scratch, clean slate sort of thing. Me and her. Did I tell you she binds books for a living . . . bookbinding. Anyway I just adore her and she just adores me and you'll just adore her too, I promise, and we're all open here aren't we? All gypsies together, and my dream is for you and Papa and Leo to come and see her for yourself. After tomorrow, 'cos tonight she's going to see the old chap and tell him everything, about me and *everything* . . . and break it off once and for all.

YVONNE (*finding it hard to speak*). So, this . . . girl . . . has been helping you out . . . with money, I mean. 'Cos you've got nothing . . . So I assume . . .

MICHAEL. Yes, she has helped me out for, I don't know, the odd meal, cigarettes, taxis . . . . But I'm happy . . . so happy. Sophie, aren't you? Happy?

YVONNE (*she turns to face him. He's horrified by her face . . .*). Happy?

MICHAEL. Oh!

YVONNE. I see – this is how you repay me. Is this why I gave birth to you, and swaddled and coddled and pampered you and loved you? And neglected my poor darling George. So some old hag, some schemer, can get her thieving claws into you and steal you from your family. It's revolting!

MICHAEL. Mama!

YVONNE. Revolting. And to let yourself get *paid* for it? There are words for that, you know.

MICHAEL. You're mad! What are you talking about? Madeleine's still young.

YVONNE. And there's the name . . .

MICHAEL. I was hardly going to conceal it.

YVONNE. And you think you can get round me, hug me and flatter *me* – no-one flatters me! – into smiling and nodding and being absolutely peachy and *happy* about my son being *kept* by the aged lover of some old woman with dyed blonde hair . . .

MICHAEL. That's not true – she doesn't dye her hair.

YVONNE. And how do you know that?

MICHAEL. . . . . And she is twenty-five years old. Do you hear? And she's never had another lover – not really – only me.

YVONNE. So now you admit it!

MICHAEL. What do you mean, I admit it? I've been trying to tell you the whole truth and nothing but the truth.

YVONNE. I'm going mad!

MICHAEL. Calm down – get back into bed.

YVONNE. Back into bed! I've been stretched out like a corpse since yesterday evening. I should never have drunk that sugar. At least I wouldn't have died of shame.

MICHAEL. What, you're talking about suicide because I'm in love with a young girl!

YVONNE. Sooner suicide than dying of shame. And don't take that tone with me. If you *were* – if you were in love with a 'young girl', if it was an affair that was clean and decent and worthy of you, and of us, then I'd probably hear you out quite calmly and happily. As it is, you can't even look me in the eyes as you unfold this disgusting, sordid saga.

MICHAEL. I forbid you.

YVONNE. You *what*?

MICHAEL (*a sudden wave of affection*). Sophie, darling, kiss me.

YVONNE. You've got lipstick all over you.

MICHAEL. It's yours!

YVONNE. I couldn't possibly kiss you – you disgust me.

MICHAEL. Sophie – that's not true.

YVONNE. Your father and I will see to it that you're not let out – you will never see this woman again. (MICHAEL *is leaning back in his chair.*) Michael, for the umpteenth time, are you trying to break that chair?

MICHAEL. I always thought of you as my best friend, my chum.

YVONNE. I am your mother, what better friend could a boy want? Anyway – how long has this business been going on?

MICHAEL. Three months.

YVONNE. Three months of lies. Disgusting.

MICHAEL. I've never lied to you. I just didn't discuss it with you.

YVONNE. Three months, of lies and deceit and clever little ploys . . . and false affection.

MICHAEL. I wanted to be as kind as possible.

YVONNE. I don't need anyone to be kind to me, thank you very much – and how dare you patronise me. You're the one we should feel sorry for!

MICHAEL. Me?

YVONNE. Yes, you. You poor little idiot, fallen hook, line and sinker into the clutches of some older woman, who probably lies about her age.

MICHAEL. But you only have to see Madeleine to . . .

YVONNE. Spare me that. And all women lie about their age. Your aunt Leonie was thirty-one for years! You don't know women.

MICHAEL. I'm beginning to get an idea.

YVONNE. And don't be rude to your mother.

MICHAEL. Sophie, my love, why should I look elsewhere when I have found a jewel. My own perfect young gorgeous gem. Would you rather I tried my luck with a woman of your age, because . . .

YVONNE. How dare you!

MICHAEL (*surprised*). How dare I what?

YVONNE. Don't answer back. I may look like a little old lady but I'm stronger than you are. And I'll have my way, just you wait and see.

MICHAEL. I think enough's been said. Otherwise we'll just say awful things – and hurt each other.

YVONNE. Oh no, no, no. Not good enough. My turn to speak now – cards on the table. And I swear to you that as long as I live you'll not marry that slut.

MICHAEL. You'll take that back!

YVONNE. I won't. Slut, slut, slut.

MICHAEL (*seizes her shoulders. She sinks to the ground*). Get up Mama. Mama!

YVONNE. Not your mama any more. An old, old woman in deep, deep pain. Who's going to scream the bloody house down. (*We hear distant banging.*) Oh good, the neighbours are banging, that's just what I want, a good old-fashioned scandal! You murderer, you vicious murderer. You've stuck the dagger in and twisted it round. Look at your eyes!

MICHAEL. Look at yours.

YVONNE. If looks could kill – you'd murder your mother.

MICHAEL. You're raving!

YVONNE. Murderer, I'm not letting you out. I'll have you arrested. I'll call the police, Yes, out the window. Why not. I'll bawl out the whole street. (*She runs downstage.*) Arrest him, arrest him!

MICHAEL (*calling*). Auntie, Auntie. Papa!

Scene Five

LEO *rushes on, embraces* YVONNE.

LEO. Yvonne, Yvonne?

    YVONNE *hits her.*

    Calm down, calm down.

MICHAEL. Quick, water. (*He runs to the bathroom, returns with water. Pointlessly.*) Papa, Papa.

YVONNE (*laughing hysterically*). Sugar solution. Shouldn't have taken it. I shouldn't have drunk it. Let me get to the window. I want to scream into the street.

LEO. Upstairs are banging again.

YVONNE. I don't give a damn.

GEORGE (*entering*). Well I do. That's the twentieth time she's complained. I don't want us to end up in the street.

YVONNE (*letting herself be led back to bed*). In the street . . . in the street . . . why not . . . who cares . . . ? None of it matters anymore. George, your son is a worm. He insulted me. He struck me.

MICHAEL (*To* GEORGE). It's not true!

GEORGE. Come to my room.

MICHAEL. I'll talk to Papa. Some things are best dealt with man to man.

They exit – MICHAEL *slams the door.*

Scene Six

YVONNE. Leo, Leo, did you hear that?

LEO. I couldn't *but* hear. But I didn't catch everything.

YVONNE. Leo, you were right. He's in love. In love with a secretary or something of the sort. He's going to leave us for her. He pushed me to the ground. His eyes are like a monster's. He doesn't love me anymore.

LEO. That doesn't follow.

YVONNE. It does. If you give it to someone, you have to take it away from someone else. That's the law of nature . . .

LEO. A boy of Michael's age has to live his own life and a mother's better off just closing her eyes to certain things. And obviously this girl's got under his skin. And I don't see what's wrong in that.

YVONNE. You don't see what's wrong? You don't see what's . . . Well perhaps you wouldn't. For a mother it's different. They get under our skins, they get into our veins, our marrow, our waters. I had him in my belly, I pushed him out of my womb. These are things you couldn't possibly understand.

LEO. That may well be. All I know is that in life one must make a huge effort to keep one's feelings under control.

YVONNE. Could you do that?

LEO. I've had to do it.

YVONNE. Well, the circumstances were obviously quite different.

LEO. The circumstances, my dear, were appalling. You may live with your head in the clouds, and you probably think it's rather endearing but your selfishness, your selfishness exceeds all imaginable limits.

YVONNE. My . . . selfishness?

LEO. What do you think I've been doing in this household for the last twenty-three years. Eh? I've been suffering, that's what. I've loved George. I still love George, and I'll probably love George until the day I die, God help me.

LEO *stops* YVONNE *interrupting with a gesture.*

When he broke off our engagement, for no particular reason, on a whim, and then decided that he'd rather marry you, and then had the incredible lack of sensitivity to actually consult me about it, I pretended to take this blow, this sledgehammer blow, lightly. To drive you away would have meant losing him, you see. And like a fool, I sacrificed myself. My life. Sounds incredible now, doesn't it, but I was young, completely obsessed, slightly mystical, a bit stupid . . .

And so I promised myself that I would serve you both, from the sidelines. And what am I now? After twenty-three years? You want to know? Your housemaid!

YVONNE. Leo. You hate me.

LEO. No. Not now. But I have. Not when George and I split up, no not then, oddly enough, then the idea of sacrifice somehow thrilled me, almost kept me alive. No, I've hated you for loving Michael too much and not loving George enough. And sometimes I've been beastly to Michael because I've blamed him for it. No, hate's not the right word. It's hard to find the precise word for what I feel about you, its a sort of emotional reflex.

But you're not basically wicked, Yvonne. You're just irresponsible – you're not quite human, you do damage without even noticing. You don't really see anything. Nothing at all. And you wander about from room to gloomy room, you moan and groan at the slightest discomfort, and you make fun of me should I ever complain about anything.

Well do you remember the 'bile beans' Michael found in my room, which you all had such a good laugh about . . . I was actually rather ill. I was bilious. Full of bile. And bile comes from anger and nerves. All this came from George. 'Cos I could tell he was tippy-toeing off somewhere like a naughty schoolboy and I was angry that you didn't have the wit to even notice – let alone try to stop him. And when Michael decided to follow in his footsteps and make a dash for the perimeter fence . . . I couldn't but tell you, to put you on your guard.

YVONNE. Rubbish. You were only too delighted to tell me. Revenge, pure and simple. An eye for an eye, a Michael for a George.

LEO. No, that's your way of thinking, your viciousness, your knife-in-the-back mentality. And I'm glad if Michael's going to marry some slut. And I'm glad if your whole ramshackle existence gets bulldozed into the dust. Great! I'm not going to lift a finger to help you. Poor George. Twenty-three years – and life is so long . . . so long . . . it's so long . . . .

GEORGE enters behind her back – she carries on, without missing a beat, and suddenly it's girl talk.

. . . .And the jacket's so short. So if you slip it off you've got the perfect evening gown which you can wear absolutely *anywhere*!

YVONNE sees GEORGE, who has entered in a state of considerable shock.

Scene Seven

GEORGE. You two seem all right. Talking dresses now? Lucky you!

YVONNE. What's the matter? You look awful.

GEORGE. I've just been listening to Michael . . .

YVONNE. And?

GEORGE. And . . . he's sorry for putting the knife in . . . he's sorry you were shouting . . . he'd like to see you.

YVONNE. Yes, that's all he's sorry about!

GEORGE. Yvonne . . . he'd like to see you . . . he's upset. Don't make him apologise or grovel or anything silly like that. It's bad enough as it is . . . I'll stay with Leo . . . I want you to go to Michael's room and just spend some time with him there alone . . . Please, Yvonne. You'd be helping Michael and you'd be helping me. I'm so tired, I'm dead on my feet.

YVONNE. I hope Michael didn't manage to talk you round.

GEORGE. Yvonne, please. It's not a matter of talking anyone round to anything. The boy's in love – that's all that matters. Don't talk about anything in particular – don't start firing questions at him, just . . . Look he's lying face down in a huge heap of old laundry. Just sit down next to him and take his hand and . . .

YVONNE (*at the door*). All right, I'll go, on one condition.

GEORGE (*softly*). Just go . . . no conditions . . .

He kisses her and steers her gently out of the room.

Scene Eight

LEO. George, you're in a state, what is it?

GEORGE. Quickly . . . Leo . . . They could come back any minute.

LEO. You're frightening me!

GEORGE. Well, my whole world's just caved in on my head.

LEO. Is it to do with Michael?

GEORGE. Yes, it's to do with Michael. My God, you could put it in the silliest Boulevard farce and it would be dismissed as being a little far-fetched.

LEO. What? Tell me! (*She shakes him.*) George. George!

GEORGE. Sorry, I was miles away. Leo – I've done something very stupid and I'm about to pay the price. Six months ago I thought I needed a typist: someone recommended someone. So that's how I met her – a young girl, beautiful, sad, simple . . . perfect.

I'd felt very alone at home. You were always running around doing something and Yvonne only really thinks about Michael. Michael. Well, to cut a very long story short I pretended I was a widower . . . under a false name of course . . . said I'd lost a daughter . . . who looked like her . . . and . . .

LEO. George, poor Georgy . . . Who could blame you? You needed some air . . . you could've . . . suffocated here.

GEORGE. So I made up more and more stories – started believing 'em myself. . . . She said she loved me . . . that youngsters were, I don't know, selfish, no use, etc, etc . . . But after three months, she changed . . . She had her sister staying with her, from the country. A married sister, terribly strict, terribly disapproving. So we couldn't keep on . . . you know . . . that's why I had to borrow a large sum of money . . . from you . . .

LEO. I knew it . . .

GEORGE. Who else could I turn to? The money you gave me to help me with my work went on the rent of a dingy basement flat. She'd visit . . . less and less frequently. Leaving me in an impossible web of lies and subterfuge, and in black despair. You can guess the rest. This mythical sister is in fact a young man, and she's in love with him. And yes, you've guessed it, it's Michael. He's just told me so himself.

LEO. Does he suspect?

GEORGE. Not a thing. He's deliriously happy, head in the clouds . . . or the sand.

LEO. And what does he want?

GEORGE. Madeleine – she's called Madeleine – had a rendez-
vous with me this evening. The purpose of which, I just
discovered from Michael, was to . . . how shall I put it . . .

LEO. To give you your marching orders . . .

GEORGE. And to tell me everything, it seems. Or rather to tell Mr
X everything – so, a clean sweep so they can both be free, for
each other. Worthy of each other. It'll break my heart, Leo, I'm
mad about her. How could it happen, in a city this size. Such a
stroke of . . . bad luck.

LEO. So what did you feel, talking to Michael?

GEORGE. Just . . . colossal embarrassment. I'm not angry with
him. It's hardly his fault, after all.

LEO. What are you going to do?

GEORGE. I thought I'd ask you. I've cancelled this evening,
obviously.

LEO. I wondered why the house had gone quiet lately. When one
of you was in the other was out. Poor George.

GEORGE. So much shame to swallow. Michael kept on saying,
'the old chap'. I know I must look absurd – but the fact is . . .
I'm really deeply hurt.

LEO (*takes his hand*). Georgy . . . I'll help you.

GEORGE. How?

LEO. You have to strike now – and hard. To get your revenge and
to put a stop to this grotesque nonsense once and for all.
Michael seems to want us all to go to her place, tomorrow. Well
fine – let's all go.

GEORGE. You're mad! Yvonne'll never agree to it.

LEO. She'll agree to it. You'll see.

GEORGE. But the *scene* – can you imagine it? When I walk in?

LEO. The girl'd sooner bite her own tongue off than breathe a
word to Michael . . .

GEORGE. When she sees me . . . She might, I don't know, faint . . .
or scream . . .

LEO. Leave it to me – it'll be fine. But hit her hard.

GEORGE. She bloody deserves it.

LEO. Get in there first. Break it off with her, and if she refuses to
break it off with Michael, threaten to spill all the beans.

GEORGE. I'm amazed – you're such a Machiavell . . .

LEO (*shyly*). I love you so much George . . . (*Jollier.*) And I want to protect your household.

GEORGE. And Yvonne, she must never, I mean never ever . . .

LEO. Shut up, she's coming . . .

GEORGE. My, what big ears you have Leo.

LEO. All the better to *stop* you getting eaten up, my dear . . .

YVONNE *enters.*

Scene Nine

GEORGE. Well? Did he say anything?

YVONNE. Not a dicky bird. I held his hand. He groaned a bit and pulled it away, and seemed to want to be alone. I'm completely destroyed. As if I'm floating. In limbo. I'm so tired. What's to become of us? Michael isn't remotely himself. He's been completely taken over by some awful, awful influence . . .

LEO. Well perhaps we ought to get to know this awful influence.

YVONNE. I know it only too well!

LEO. Do you really think we can stop these children seeing each other?

YVONNE. Children?

LEO. Oh come on Yvonne, Michael and his girl . . .

YVONNE. Leo, what are you talking about, 'girl'? It's plainly some woman who'll sleep with absolutely anybody. A woman, God knows how old, who behaves as if butter wouldn't melt in her mouth, who's completely fooled Mickey, who now thinks the sun shines out of her . . .

LEO. All the more reason to disabuse him.

YVONNE. I'm relying on George to show some strength of character for once and to strike now . . . while . . .

GEORGE. . . . the iron is hot? That old cliché?

YVONNE. Be a proper father to the boy. Now, supposing that there's some truth in all this and this woman does want to leave her . . . sugar daddy . . . and supposing she is serious about marrying Mickey, then it's your duty to stop him taking on such a ludicrous responsibility. How was he expecting to keep her?

GEORGE. He told me he was fed up with doing nothing. That he'd decided to work.

YVONNE. To live off our money. Or rather your money.

LEO. The little I have is yours, you know that . . .

YVONNE. But not hers. No, I can see everything quite, quite clearly now. My head's . . . it's essential for George to put a stop to the whole thing. Leo, you tell him . . . Just put your foot down and *forbid* it.

LEO. Have you ever seen that work with people who're in love . . . ?

YVONNE. You're *un*believable, both of you. I've known him for twenty-two years. And some minx from the gutter isn't going to turn him inside out in three measly months.

GEORGE. Not in three months. No . . . in three minutes. That's what love does to you.

YVONNE. Ridiculous. If I were a man I'd know exactly what to say to her.

LEO. But that's what Michael wants. For you to talk to her.

YVONNE. He expects me to obey his orders?

GEORGE. Who said anything about orders? Come on, Yvonne, don't let's be melodramatic.

YVONNE. No, let me work this out . . . you and George are seriously suggesting . . .

GEORGE. I'm not suggesting anything.

YVONNE. Well then you're presenting, as a real possibility, that I might go with George to actually see . . . visit . . . this . . . woman, with Leo bringing up the rear . . .

GEORGE. Just a recce, to size up the opposition . . .

YVONNE. So. Off we trot *en famille*, like a Christmas visit, all smiles and Cherry Brandy . . .

LEO. You haven't thought it through yet Yvonne. Can you really imagine living with a Michael who lies to you from morning to night? Can you imagine living without Michael at all?

YVONNE. Shut up.

LEO. Him leaving home altogether?

YVONNE. Shut up, shut up.

LEO. It'd be so much easier to use a bit of cunning to win him back, and to earn some gratitude from him into the bargain.

YVONNE. We mustn't deceive Mickey. It'd only make matters worse when he finds out.

LEO. It's for his own good, Yvonne. And you're quite free to give the marriage your blessing if you find her to be . . . a gem, as Mickey says.

GEORGE. Look Yvonne. If you think about it, calmly, Leo's plan isn't as crazy as it sounds.

YVONNE. No, no, no, no. Stop it. I'm always giving in, I *hate* myself for giving in. And I am not setting foot in that woman's house.

LEO (*stopping* YVONNE *wandering round the room*). One more thing, Yvonne. The worst thing, I think, is not even being able to imagine where they go when they go, our loved ones. Where are they now? What are they up to? Aren't you even curious about her, about this creature who hurts you so much, but hasn't got a shape or a face? Wouldn't you like to reach out and *touch* the hurt? Prod it a bit and see how it feels? If something of yours is stolen, wouldn't you like to be able to visualise its whereabouts?

YVONNE. It's with her . . . that little thief.

LEO. Well, you can go and *see* the thief, Yvonne. You can go and reclaim your stolen property. You can go with George. And I'll be there with you.

YVONNE *slumps on the bed. Only her physical posture indicates her acquiescence.*

GEORGE. I always admire you, Yvonne. You're always much stronger than one'd think.

YVONNE. Or much weaker.

LEO. It takes courage to leave your dark old room and go out into the sunlight.

YVONNE. If that's the sunlight, I'd rather stay in the dark.

LEO. You must be fantastically careful how you put this to Mickey. He could easily smell a rat.

GEORGE. Leo, go and get him . . . Tell him you've got a lovely surprise for him. He likes surprises.

LEO. Be brave . . .

She exits.

Scene Ten

YVONNE. This is a nightmare.

GEORGE. You're telling me!

YVONNE. If we go and see this . . . person – I'll slip off somewhere with Leonie while you talk to her.

GEORGE. All right, I promise I'll speak to her in private.

YVONNE. Don't make me, I'd only start screaming at her . . . I'm not in the habit of talking to that class of woman.

GEORGE. Nor'm I, my love. And at our age new habits are hard to acquire.

LEO *pushes* MICHAEL *into the room. He's in disarray – very defensive.*

Scene Eleven

LEO. Go on . . .

GEORGE. Come in Michael.

MICHAEL. What do you want?

GEORGE. Your mother will tell you.

MICHAEL *enters,* LEO *shuts the door.*

YVONNE (*talking with some effort*). Mickey – I was harsh with you. You were being honest with me and I was being ghastly. And I'm sorry. Your father's been wonderful. He's talked to me, Mickey darling, and we don't wish you any harm, you know that. On the contrary. We want the best for you. And I hate being beastly or unfair. What you asked of us is almost impossible.

MICHAEL. But . . .

GEORGE. Don't interrupt your mother.

YVONNE. But this almost impossible step you want us to take, we've decided, Mickey, to take it. This we will do. For you, my darling.

MICHAEL. Sophie! Papa! I can't believe it. It's *un*believable!

GEORGE. Well, it's true. Now Michael, we'd like you to convey our best wishes to her and say that we would be delighted to pay her a visit tomorrow.

MICHAEL. I'm dreaming, I'm dreaming, this is amazing. Papa, how can I thank you, Mama.

He goes to embrace YVONNE, *she turns away.*

YVONNE. It isn't us you must thank – it's your aunt.

MICHAEL. You, Aunt Leo. Thank you.

MICHAEL *whirls* LEO *round in his arms. He puts her down.*

LEO. Don't thank me, thank all of us. Thank the whole gypsy camp.

Curtain.

ACT TWO

Scene One

We are in MADELEINE'*s flat. A staircase* (*spiral?*) *leads to an upper level. It's very tidy. Several shelves of similarly bound books.* MICHAEL *has come in from the bathroom.*

MADELEINE. That's unbelievable.

MICHAEL. Everyone says that at home. Just like that, same stress, 'unbelievable'. I don't know if I brought it here or if I got if off you. Mama'd hit the roof if she thought she'd picked anything up off you!

MADELEINE. I don't think I pronounce . . . that word any differently from anybody else, do I?

MICHAEL. Nobody says it like that but you, my love. Except now everybody does, Mama, Papa, Aunt Leo, they all say 'My God, that's *un*believable'. Just like you.

MADELEINE. Your mother will never believe you came here to have a bath. She'll think you're doing it to irritate her, to show her you're more at home here than at home.

MICHAEL. It's all Aunt Leo's fault. Our bath's all blocked up and that's her department. Aunt Leo is cleanliness and hygiene incarnate. I'm sure you'll get on famously.

MADELEINE. My bathtub's not blocked. Come on, hurry up.

MICHAEL. You're so like Aunt Leo – every inch the diplomat.

MADELEINE. It's your cleanness I love.

MICHAEL. No-one's ever called me clean before.

MADELEINE. You're never really dirty – you're more grubby, like kids are grubby. You know, like kid's knees. Just need a good old scrub. Deep down you're as clean as a whistle.

MICHAEL. I'm hopeless and messy and a dunce, and you know it.

MADELEINE. Oh yes, and what does that make me?

MICHAEL. The wise woman of the woods. All those books you've read. All those classics.

MADELEINE. I just bind them, I don't read them. Not all of them.

MICHAEL. You could easily make a living out of your bookbinding. Then I could live off you.

MADELEINE. You'll be out working, my boy. Play your cards right you can work for me and one day we'll open a shop.

MICHAEL. And we'll be rich, and then we'll buy a house.

MADELEINE. A flat, Mickey. Why do you always say a house?

MICHAEL. That's what we say at home. A house. This is the house, walk round the house. We even say 'go upstairs to bed' and we haven't got an upstairs.

MADELEINE. That's *un*believable.

MICHAEL. If this were our house – the studio up there would be down here, and *vice versa* and everything would be scrunched together in the most unholy mess. I can't help it. Inanimate objects follow me about, like cats. How do you do it?

MADELEINE. It's just order. You either have a sense of it or you don't. Like an ear for music or a head for heights.

MICHAEL *has found his socks underneath* MADELEINE.

MICHAEL. Look where my socks have got to. I was certain I left them upstairs.

MADELEINE. In the living-room. No, you took them off down here.

MICHAEL. Living-room! The very word sounds exotic. There's no such thing in our house. Every room's a living-sleeping-working-having-a nervous breakdown room. Sophie's looks like a battlefield. Sometimes it's just that – wars break out, the neighbours bang on the walls – boom, boom, – and then there's an uneasy truce.

MADELEINE. And your father puts up with all that?

MICHAEL. Oh Papa; Papa thinks he's inventing new wonders of the world. In fact he's working on the underwater sub-machine gun. Shooting real bullets – underwater. He thinks Jules Verne's the world's greatest writer. He's about ten years younger than me.

MADELEINE. And your mother?

MICHAEL. When I was little I wanted to marry Mama. Papa said, 'You're far too young'. And I said, apparently, 'Don't worry, I'll wait till I'm older than her'.

MADELEINE. Sweet.

MICHAEL. Sorry to bore you with my family history. It's just that I didn't want to tell you too much about them till I'd told them all about you. Sophie was fine about it, and Papa, *and* Aunt Leonie. At the beginning, though, it was a real drama.

MADELEINE. What do you mean?

MICHAEL. Mama wanted to call the police and have me arrested.

MADELEINE. Arrested. That's . . .

BOTH. *Un*believable.

They laugh.

MADELEINE. Whose fault was it?

MICHAEL. Mine. Yours. Ours. I couldn't resist spending the
    night here. And the next day . . . the next day . . .

MADELEINE. The next day you were a complete nervous wreck.

MICHAEL. I was.

MADELEINE. I told you a hundred times, ring home.

MICHAEL. For God's sake don't say that in front of Sophie.
    You'd really be putting your foot in it.

MADELEINE. Excuse me, hark who's talking. You can't open
    your mouth without putting your foot in it.

MICHAEL. True.

MADELEINE. And I love you all the more for that, you silly ass.
    You can't even lie properly.

MICHAEL. It's too complicated. I'd always forget what lie I'd
    told to whom.

MADELEINE. Me, I hate lies. The slightest hint of a lie makes me
    feel sick.

MICHAEL (*having tied one shoe*). I'm a shoe short.

MADELEINE. Look for it.

MICHAEL. *Un*believable. One minute it's . . .

MADELEINE. Go on. Party games. Hunt the slipper.

MICHAEL (*on all fours*). You've seen it haven't you?

MADELEINE. *Ages* ago. It's staring you in the face!

MICHAEL (*moving away from the table, on the top of which is the
    missing shoe*). Am I warm?

MADELEINE. Freezing!

MICHAEL. I thought you wanted me to hurry up. (*She shows him
    the shoe.*) You're no fun, Mama would have hidden it in my
    bed.

MADELEINE. She sounds adorable, your mother. Such a pity that
    I'm scared witless.

MICHAEL (*putting his shoe on*). She thinks she's ugly and she's not, she's beautiful; even more beautiful than she would be if she *were* beautiful. She'll come as a thirty-one year old. And it's entirely possible, oh God!, she'll have got her best fur out of mothballs . . .

MADELEINE. I'm so scared.

MICHAEL. They're the ones who'll be scared. But Aunt Leo will break the ice – she's brilliant at all that.

MADELEINE. Do you always go out all together?

MICHAEL (*naïvely*). Sophie never goes out anywhere. Papa goes out, quite a lot actually, and Leo goes out to do shopping and all that. Running the household's a full-time job. And I go out, to see my girlfriend who I'm in love with.

MADELEINE. Do you love me?

MICHAEL. Look. (*He turns to a mirror.*) What do you think? Here I am, all done up like a dog's dinner, in my 'will you marry me' outfit. Damn!

MADELEINE. What?

MICHAEL. I should have got my hair cut.

MADELEINE. It's Monday. All the hairdressers will be shut.

MICHAEL. How do you manage to know that?

MADELEINE. That the hairdressers'll be shut? Well . . .

MICHAEL. No, that it's Monday. (*Kisses her.*) I only know it's Sunday 'cos the daily doesn't do Sundays and I have to help in the kitchen.

MADELEINE. That's not how you know it's Sunday. People have got time on their hands on Sunday. It's sort of disordered – and always sad somehow.

MICHAEL. It's all order and disorder for you isn't it?

MADELEINE. Which are they expecting to find here?

MICHAEL. They're expecting the worst, I fear. A little old lady with dyed hair.

MADELEINE. Well, they're not far wrong. I'm miles older than you.

MICHAEL. Three years. They'll be flabbergasted.

MADELEINE. Let's hope so; in the right way, at least.

MICHAEL (*taking her in his arms*). Maddy bear, you'll wind them round your little finger. You know you will. If only . . .

MADELEINE. No, what?

MICHAEL. It's just . . . if only the other business had been cleared up – I mean sorted out. So there was no difficulty, no ambiguity.

MADELEINE. You know I was going to . . . he 'phoned and put it off.

MICHAEL. Just bad luck, I suppose.

MADELEINE. I'll sort it all out tomorrow.

MICHAEL. You look a bit relieved . . .

MADELEINE. I am a bit, to be honest. When George postponed it I didn't protest, put it that way.

MICHAEL. George, that's my papa's name.

MADELEINE. I don't know which appointment worries me more – the meeting with George the First, or the one with George your father. They're both pretty scary.

MICHAEL. You don't love him, do you?

MADELEINE. Yes Michael, I do.

MICHAEL. You do love him . . .

MADELEINE. Look, life isn't as simple as you'd like it to be. The fact is, I love only you, but I still love him.

MICHAEL. I don't get it.

MADELEINE. If I didn't love him, Michael, I wouldn't be worthy of loving you. Or, more precisely, I wouldn't be capable of loving you. I'd be dead. I was on the brink of suicide, he saved me . . .

MICHAEL. Well that's gratitude.

MADELEINE. No, Michael, it's more than gratitude.

MICHAEL. I just don't understand.

MADELEINE. Well perhaps you wouldn't. Bless you, you're so much in your own little world. I didn't love him enough to find real love. Not like I did with you. I loved him enough to hide things from him. I love him enough to feel sick with fear at what I've got to do now. To shoot him dead at point blank range.

MICHAEL. *Un*believable.

MADELEINE. Look Mickey, be fair. Put yourself in his shoes. I'm everything to him. He's a widower . . . Lost his daughter. I look like she did. You're asking me to sign his death warrant. He doesn't think I'm capable of lying . . .

MICHAEL. Well in that case hang on to him, keep him, why not? Easy! I'll just ring up the family and head 'em off at the pass . . .

MADELEINE. Don't be silly. I've said I'll do it, and I'll do it. And I'll do it because when you're in love you'll do anything – kill someone, tear their guts out – anything. It's all decided. We won't talk about it any more . . .

MICHAEL. I want to talk about it. Look . . . if it was the same thing . . . with Mama . . . if it came to that . . . I wouldn't think twice.

MADELEINE. You *would* think twice. Which is why I adore you. And it's not the same thing. Your mother's got your father, your aunt.

MICHAEL. No, she's only got me.

MADELEINE. In that case she must hate me.

MICHAEL. No-one could hate you, my love. And Mama'll love you too, when she sees that you're like a part of me, that we're really just one person.

MADELEINE. You shouldn't have told her about . . . him.

MICHAEL. Sophie's told me so often that she's my best friend, I could hardly hide anything from her, could I?

MADELEINE. You hid *me* from her. And our love.

MICHAEL. That was only because of *him*, and I wanted them to see you as brave, and free, and for there to be nothing . . . dubious . . . You know, all above board.

MADELEINE. No, you did the right thing. If you start being honest, you've got to go the whole hog.

MICHAEL. That's right. That's what'll give you courage tomorrow.

MADELEINE. Please, I don't even want to talk about it. And if it hurts, think of it this way, I was as fond of George as I would be of your father, as I will be of your father when I meet him.

MICHAEL. But . . .

MADELEINE. Hush.

MICHAEL. Are you angry with me?

MADELEINE. I'd be angry with you if you weren't jealous. I'd be angry with you if you were jealous. I'd be angry with you if you weren't angry with me. I'd be really angry with you if you weren't angry about being angry with me.

MICHAEL. Oh, stop it! Look they're lovely, they're generosity itself. I mean the fact they're coming at all . . . !

MADELEINE. It terrifies me that they're coming at all. It's all a bit too easy, too pat. You said your mother didn't want to hear my name mentioned. And one minute later she changes her mind. That really terrifies me.

MICHAEL. They fly off the handle and they scream and they shout and they slam doors – then Aunt Leo calms them down and they listen to her advice. She is the Guardian Angel, hovering above the camp. She's very beautiful, very elegant, very direct. She criticises our disorder but deep down she couldn't do without it.

Ring at the doorbell.

MADELEINE. They're here. Look, I'm going, All right? I'm going to go upstairs.

MICHAEL. Don't leave me here alone!

MADELEINE. You can come up and fetch me.

MICHAEL. Madeleine!

MADELEINE. It's best.

She goes up.

Scene Two

MICHAEL. Aunt Leo! Where are the others? Are they still coming?

LEO. Don't worry, they're coming. I arranged it so I could be here early.

MICHAEL. You are good.

LEO. It's tidy.

MICHAEL (*laughing*). Yes, that's me actually, I tidied up specially.

LEO. Likely story. Where's your girlfriend?

MICHAEL. In her studio, where she does her work, her bookbinding. (*He indicates the staircase.*)

LEO (*looking out, downstage*). It looks out on to the park. Nice. That's what your mother could do with, instead of the block opposite and those ghastly street lights.

MICHAEL. Now don't you be rude about the gypsy camp. My room looks out onto a courtyard and I'm fond of my courtyard.

LEO. Why don't you call her?

MICHAEL. Madeleine, Maddy . . . No point, you can't hear up there.

LEO. That's handy.

MICHAEL. Why?

LEO. Well your father's taking all this very well, and he's got a very clear idea of what's to be done. He feels he has to talk to your friend on their own – he doesn't want your mother listening and butting in. When we come down, it'll all be seen to.

MICHAEL. You're an angel. (*He kisses her.*) I'll go and get her for you.

He bounds up the stairs. LEO, left alone, looks into the bathroom, shuts the door, looks at the books. MICHAEL steers MADELEINE down the stairs, pushing her by the shoulders.

Scene Three

LEO. How do you do?

MICHAEL. I told you it was just her. You needn't be frightened of Auntie Leo. She's only the advance guard!

MADELEINE. Madame . . .

LEO offers her hand, MADELEINE takes it.

LEO. Mademoiselle, you are extremely pretty . . .

MADELEINE. Madame – you're exactly as Michael said you'd be.

MICHAEL. I said you had a squint, a hump and a moustache!

MADELEINE. He said you were very beautiful, and very elegant . . .

LEO. And very orderly. But I see I'm not alone in that.

MADELEINE. I hate disorder.

LEO. Well, good luck with Michael.

MICHAEL. And Sophie and Papa are coming along after?

LEO. We agreed to meet here. Your mother didn't like it. I pretended I had something to buy. But in fact I wanted to get

here first and prepare the ground. So. Now we're all in it together. Fellow conspirators. I love your upstairs. I was worried there'd only be one room.

MADELEINE. No, it's an old attic, actually two which they knocked through to make flats, well, flats plus studio. And that's the staircase.

LEO. And when you're up there can you hear what's going on down here?

MADELEINE. Why?..

MICHAEL. Did you hear me calling you just now?

MADELEINE. No.

LEO. It's very important. They'll be here soon. We must try and make it work. You know what your mother's like. We'll go upstairs together. Michael can walk up and down and shout. You lead the way.

MICHAEL. No you do it, recite something dramatic. (*Finds book.*) *Britannicus*?

LEO. You can't bellow out Racine, it's far too good for that. (*Finds another book.*) Ah, *Lorenzaccio,* that will do.

Ready? Here goes

– Assassins, I am done for. My throat is cut.

– Die you dog, die, die.

He stamps his foot. (*She stamps her foot.*)

– Hey, archers, come hither. Help me, I am dead, Lorenzo the Devil.

–– Die you cur. I'll run you through you, you varlet. His heart, tear out his heart. And now his damn-ed guts. Let us rend him into pieces, and eat him, eat him up.'

During this MICHAEL has tiptoed back down the stairs.

MICHAEL (*applauding wildly*). Bravo.

LEO. Michael, you weren't up there.

MICHAEL. I was. We got bored, I couldn't hear.

LEO. Good.

MICHAEL. You were terrific. You could easily've been an actress.

MADELEINE *joins him, they come down together.*

MADELEINE. You were brilliant. And I didn't even see you.

LEO. Your mother can be quite an actress too, when occasion demands.

Ring at the doorbell.

(*To* MADELEINE) Quick, upstairs. And remember, I've only just arrived. I don't know you, I haven't seen you yet, understood? Because you, Michael, wouldn't let me see her yet. Got that? Now let them in. Your mother first.

Another ring.

Scene Four

Voices off.

GEORGE. You took your time! I thought we'd come to the wrong flat!

YVONNE. Is there not a maid?

MICHAEL. No Mother, the same as at home. Aunt Leo – did *you* hear them ringing?

They enter.

YVONNE. Is Leo here?

LEO. I've only just got here. You almost bumped into me on the landing.

YVONNE. Have you been here long?

LEO. I said, I only just arrived.

MICHAEL. Aunt Leo thought she was late and that you'd be here already.

YVONNE. Is it . . . just you?

MICHAEL. Madeleine's upstairs in her studio – where she does her book binding.

YVONNE. What luxury!

MICHAEL. It's tidy.

YVONNE (*to* MICHAEL). It's not exactly your style, is it?

MICHAEL. Well, give me a chance. I'm not here often enough. If I lived with Madeleine . . . or if I visited an awful lot, then I think I'd win the battle . . . disorder would prevail.

GEORGE. Michael, shouldn't you inform her we're here.

MICHAEL. Yes, of course. Oh Papa, don't be so stiff and formal. And Sophie, sit down. All of you sit down. Relax. Try and look natural. Leo, you see to them. Madeleine's hopeless at all that, she'll be stiff as a clothes horse and frighten you all off.

GEORGE. I'm not sure you appreciate the seriousness of this visit, my boy. You seem to be treating it rather flippantly.

LEO. He's just trying to break the ice.

MICHAEL. You'll make me cry.

YVONNE. Now, Leo, George is really upset about this. It's one of those family moments: father, mother and son. And not to be taken lightly.

LEO. It's funny that you start becoming conventional parents the minute matters start getting ever so slightly unconventional. I think Michael's being very brave and very decent. Go and find your little girl.

YVONNE. If we can call her that.

MICHAEL (*at the stairs*). Look, my whole happiness is at stake here. So please, for the last time. I ask you to be nice and warm and helpful to Madeleine – and not to give her the cold shoulder.

YVONNE. But darling, nothing could be further from our wishes.

MICHAEL. Sophie, Papa, Leo – please help me – my nerves are in shreds.

LEO. Of course we'll help you. We're all just anxious, that's why we're all putting on a bit of an act. It'll all be fine, I promise. Now, off you go.

MICHAEL. Righty-ho.

He does so.

Scene Five

YVONNE (*to* GEORGE). You look even worse than I feel.

GEORGE. Now, now children, Let's all sit down. No, I'll stand over here, opposite Yvonne.

Tableau.

Scene Six

MICHAEL (*talking over his shoulder*). Smile!

He reveals MADELEINE who comes down, still seeing nothing.

MADELEINE. Madame.

YVONNE gets up and approaches her. GEORGE stays on his own.

MICHAEL. This is my mama . . .

Silence.

YVONNE. But you're charming, mademoiselle. And so young . . . more like a little girl. May I ask how old you are?

MADELEINE. I am twenty-five. But you also . . .

She notices GEORGE, her voice changes.

My God. What are you doing here. Who let you in? (*Turns to the women.*)

This gentleman . . . is . . .

MICHAEL. . . . . Is my father. That's who. And Papa, this is Madeleine.

MADELEINE. Your . . . father?

MICHAEL. You see. Always happens. No-one ever believes he's old enough to be *anyone's* father. If we went out on the town together everyone would think we were chums. So here we all are, the full complement. The raggle taggle gypsies *en bloc*. We're not as bad as all that, are we? Are you all right?

MADELEINE. Yes . . . I'm fine.

YVONNE. Don't try and get up. Leo, see to her. Michael, can you show us round the flat. I'm dying to see what this upstairs looks like.

MICHAEL. But . . .

YVONNE. You lead the way, Leo and I will follow.

GEORGE. Shall I . . . (*Makes as if to join them.*)

YVONNE. No, you stay here.

MICHAEL. There's a thermos of hot tea upstairs. And three cups. You see, we think of everything.

YVONNE starts up the stairs, LEO follows, MICHAEL kisses MADELEINE, and turns to join them.

MADELEINE. Are you leaving me on my own?

MICHAEL. Not at all. Papa's here.

MADELEINE. No, you mustn't. Don't leave me on my own. Please, Michael, please . . .

YVONNE. Michael!

MADELEINE. Madame . . . please . . . I'll come up with you . . . and serve the tea.

YVONNE. We'll manage. Michael can help us.

GEORGE. Please stay here, mademoiselle. I promised Michael I'd speak to you – and I promised my wife, who is considerably more nervous than myself, that I'd speak to you in private.

YVONNE (*top of the stairs*). Hurry up George.

MADELEINE. Madame, please, another woman . . .

YVONNE. Really! Some women make a fuss about nothing!

MICHAEL. Go on, use your charm. See if you can't win him round. But don't you two go running off together!

He exits.

Scene Seven

GEORGE. Well, here we are . . .

MADELEINE. This is monstrous.

GEORGE. As you say, monstrous. *Un*believable. But there it is. (*He taps the backs of the books on the shelves.*) It's a work of art – a masterpiece – the equal of any of these. It could be out of one of them, it probably is; that's why we read books, isn't it, to see if we're in there somewhere. Only these (*Looking at them.*) are mostly tragedies, and this is a comedy, isn't it, a farce and I'm the hero. And by now, by Act Two I should be getting big big laughs.

You know they say . . . man deceived – funny, older man deceived by younger man – very funny, older man deceived by own son – rolling in the aisles. It's classic comedy. It's perfect, it's Molière. And if it didn't happen in real life, he'd never have put it in his plays. So we're classic characters. Aren't you proud? You should be, Maddy.

MADELEINE. George!

GEORGE Can they hear us from up there, Maddy?

MADELEINE. Please don't call me that and you know full well that we can't be heard.

GEORGE. Of course. You locked me up there twice, the first two times your sister came to visit . . . And she, of course, was Michael, wasn't she?

MADELEINE. Yes.

GEORGE. Better and better. So afterwards it was more convenient to get me to rent a flat. Why did you carry on? Why did you lie? I thought the merest *hint* of a lie made you physically sick. You seem to be quite cured now. Why didn't you tell me the truth?

MADELEINE. You wouldn't have believed me if I had.

GEORGE. You've just been lying and lying and lying through your perfect little teeth.

MADELEINE. And what about you? You didn't trust me with the truth. You lied as much as I did. Why? Tell me.

GEORGE. I was suffocating at home. I was going mad. I was so alone, so empty. So I decided to sublimate my loneliness, to turn it into something real. And I invented a sad lonely man who had every reason to be as sad and lonely as me. When I was with you here, in our house, I was in another world, quite free, and I forgot everything, even Michael. And I kept my two worlds quite separate.

MADELEINE. If only you'd told me your real name.

GEORGE. You'd still have met Michael.

MADELEINE. I wouldn't have let it get this far.

GEORGE. Oh come on. The only difference would've been that I'd have received my marching orders three months earlier. So why weren't you honest with me?

MADELEINE. George. I lied to make everything better . . . because I loved you . . . because I love you.

GEORGE. You're *un*believable.

MADELEINE. Please let me finish. I gave you everything I could. You talked to me of the daughter you had lost. You were good to me. You weren't like other men. I was a wreck. You threw me a life line. Of course I clung to you, what else could I do? I held you fast with all my heart . . .

GEORGE. All I want to know is, did you love me? I loved you, I worshipped you, and thousands and thousands of times I'd ask you, 'Do you love me', adding 'you can't possibly', but you always said, 'No Georgy, I do love you, I do'. Was that another lie?

MADELEINE. You bombarded me with question after question, always ending up with 'do you love me?', and I'd say 'Of course, I love you, you know I love you . . . lots and lots'. And then you'd get angry and badger me and beg me just to say the words – and in the end I'd give in, to please you, and say it, and say 'Yes I do. I love you'.

GEORGE. You didn't *have* to say it.

MADELEINE. You were stubborn. I tried everything to open your eyes – and you just refused to see.

GEORGE. It was too late, damn you. I was in 'too deep'. If you'd said, 'I don't love you, but I'll try to love you, you must be patient', I would've at least known where I was. But you led me out onto the quicksands and stood and watched me sink. Until this new love arrived out of nowhere. And then I was just in the way.

MADELEINE. That's not true. I just didn't want to hurt you, that's all, and I didn't know how not to. Breaking up with you was torture to me. I said as much to Michael – which only goes to show how much I love him.

GEORGE. Do you love Michael?

MADELEINE. Are you asking for yourself or for him?

GEORGE. I'm asking as his father.

MADELEINE. Yes, I love him. He's mine. He's *me*. I can't imagine life without him. Misery grinds you down – you expect very little – I certainly didn't expect love. I mean proper love, love greater than yours and mine. And if I led you a merry dance, I'm sorry – it's just that it took Michael to show me that there was love and there was *love* – and that, actually, I had a right to be happy. I'd just never dreamed it could be possible. *Un*believable.

GEORGE. Does Michael love you?

MADELEINE. You can find that out for yourself. If he knew, if he knew the truth, he'd hate you, he'd kill me, he'd die of it.

GEORGE. There's no question of him finding out.

MADELEINE. You're such a good man, George. I knew you'd understand, I knew that after the initial shock you'd understand that Michael's happiness had to come first.

GEORGE. *Michael's* happiness . . . ??

MADELEINE. I'll thank you every day of my life!

GEORGE. I'm sorry, do you really think I'm just going to give Michael to you? Just like that, on a plate?

MADELEINE. What?

GEORGE. You surely don't think I'm going to allow this, do you?

MADELEINE. You're . . . not serious . . . you're not going to take him away?

GEORGE. What did you think? That I was going to just step aside, and give you both my blessing and spend the rest of my days watching you . . . whooping it up in each other's arms?

MADELEINE. You're mad. It's your son. Your son's happiness. Michael's happiness.

GEORGE. How could he be happy with a woman who lies and cheats, isn't even faithful. You cheated me, you cheated him, how many others are there? There's probably a third, or a fourth.

MADELEINE. George, stop it, you don't know what you're saying.

GEORGE. You're right. I don't.

MADELEINE. I knew it.

GEORGE. But even so, since there isn't anybody else why not invent someone?

MADELEINE. What do you mean?

GEORGE. Yes, that's it we must invent a young man, someone your own age, a bit older than Michael, and yes you were hiding him because you were ashamed, but you're obsessed with him and you can't let go of him, and he's desperate to marry you.

MADELEINE. Is this a joke? Is this some sort of test?

GEORGE. I've never been more serious in my life.

MADELEINE. But what you're suggesting is . . . criminal!

GEORGE. Do it, Maddy, or I'll tell everything.

MADELEINE. What, you wouldn't tell your son, your wife . . . ?

GEORGE. What I say to my wife is no business of yours. Anyway I've decided to tell her everything, come what may.

MADELEINE. Then she'll tell him.

GEORGE. Only if you force her to, by not giving Michael up.

MADELEINE. To commit this . . . abortion and just wash your hands of it. Because *you* mustn't expect to ever see me again.

GEORGE. My dear girl, I wouldn't wish to.. I'm cured, and now I intend to cure my son as well.

MADELEINE. Of what? Love?

GEORGE. Love . . . love . . . what's that? Just a four letter word.
No, I merely intend to dissuade him from a marriage which
circumstances have rendered quite unacceptable.

MICHAEL (*voice off*). Have you finished? Can we come down
yet?

GEORGE (*shouts up to him*). Not yet. We're getting on famously
– like we've known each other for ages.

MICHAEL. That's wonderful.

He slams the door.

MADELEINE. George, just now I was in a dream world, a world
in which no-one could ever take Michael from me. But hearing
his voice reminded me that he *does* exist. He exists in the real
world, in a ghastly world, a world in which people want to
harm him and to take him away from me. And I'm going to
damn well fight to hang on to him, and to keep him forever.

GEORGE. I've been thinking too, Madeleine. And I think you
should be free. So I think I'll just tell him. So then he'll know
who the other man really is . . . he'll know everything. It means
I'll lose him of course . . . but then again so will you.

MADELEINE. George, George, listen to me – you have to believe
me.

GEORGE. Believe you? Do you think I'm that naïve?

MADELEINE. Yes, naïve and good and noble. Everything I love
in you. Everything I adore in Michael. Don't be a monster, don't
become a monster. Haven't you punished me enough, by
turning up like that, out of the blue, frightening me half to
death? You could have killed me, I could so easily have given
everything away.

GEORGE. I wasn't worried. I knew that if you really adored
Michael you'd somehow manage to contain yourself. Which
you did.

MADELEINE. Aha, you see, you know I adore him.

GEORGE. Look, this marriage is quite absurd. It is not the life I
would wish for my son – he should stay in his own milieu.

MADELEINE. Which milieu is that . . . ? I'd love to know. My
father was a workman, as was his father before him. I was born
tough. And I mean to change Michael. He'll learn to work. He's
changing already. Your 'milieu' only teaches him dabbling and
idleness. Michael's a child. And you're a child too, George.
Someone's broken your nice toy, so you want to break theirs.

That's all I was really, your toy, your plaything. Nothing much to you. But everything to Michael. He needs me. You've got all the things you chose to hide from me. A wife, a family – you're the head of a household. How can you compare our affair, which was based on a false premise, on a false name, a false address, your false loneliness, to the real feelings of a real person who really loves me heart and soul?

GEORGE. His mother will never agree to it.

MADELEINE. Do you both hate me?

GEORGE That's what kids say when you stop them climbing trees.

MADELEINE. What about his aunt?

GEORGE. She loved me . . . once . . . when she was a girl . . . Perhaps she still loves me, secretly. So she will hate you if, through any of your doing, I am made to look ridiculous or to suffer in any way.

MADELEINE. No she won't. She'll see me loving Michael and she'll see Michael loving me, and if we have children . . .

GEORGE. What? To spawn children from an unholy bloody mess like this . . . what an abomination!

MADELEINE. George, stop it, you're drifting away from me, you're changing. Be proper, be fair, be yourself.

GEORGE. I know what I'm doing, I know what I'm saying. You have to give him back. We have to invent this other man. So, you decide, should I tell him that lie, or the truth?

MADELEINE. That is so contemptible.

GEORGE. I'm only doing my duty.

MADELEINE. You're a madman.

GEORGE. I'm a father.

MADELEINE. Nonsense – you're not a father, you're just a selfish brute, a pathetic jilted fool who's trying to get his own back.

GEORGE. I forbid you to speak like that!

MADELEINE. Liar, selfish pathetic liar. (*He pushes her off.*) Yes, that's right, hit back. Don't pretend it's because of your son's happiness. Your revenge isn't against me, it's against him. You couldn't give a damn about his well being. You're just jealous. And that's all that matters to you.

GEORGE. There's not much time. You tell him your story or I'll tell him the truth.

MADELEINE. Go ahead.

GEORGE. Very well. I trust you've fully considered all the implications . . .

MADELEINE. No, no, don't, I didn't mean it. If he doesn't know, there's still a hope, even if he leaves me . . . but if he knows – then it's all over.

GEORGE. You see . . .

MADELEINE. I won't have the strength.

GEORGE. I'll be here to help you.

MADELEINE. This is unbearable.

GEORGE. Oh yes? And how bearable do you think it was for me having to hear Michael yesterday? Telling me you were his mistress, all the sordid details, hearing myself described as the old chap.

MADELEINE. He was so proud of you – of your youth . . .

GEORGE You were my youth, you were my last hope.

MADELEINE. So be generous. It's his turn now. Step aside for him – and for me.

GEORGE. This is not a personal matter. I merely wish to safeguard my son's future happiness.

MADELEINE. Give me more time.

GEORGE. How much more time do you want? They've been waiting up there for ages. Decide. Now.

Silence.

All right, time's up . . . I'll tell them everything.

Goes to stairs.

MADELEINE (*screams*). No!!

GEORGE. You'll do what we agreed?

MADELEINE. Yes.

GEORGE. You swear?

MADELEINE. Yes.

GEORGE. Swear it on Michael.

MADELEINE. Yes.

GEORGE. 'I solemnly swear . . . '

MADELEINE. ' . . . on Michael.' You bastard.

GEORGE. I'm a father who's trying to prevent his son from falling into the same trap he did.

MADELEINE. I'm not the type of person who'll try to kill themselves and fail, and try again. I'm not that sort. But I *will* die of this, slowly, of despair, and of disgust.

GEORGE. No. You'll live. And you'll work . . . And you'll forget Michael.

MADELEINE. Never.

GEORGE. So. Shall we tell him our little story?

MADELEINE. As long as he never knows the truth.

GEORGE. I'll go and get him.

MADELEINE. George, no, please. Wait, wait just a moment.

GEORGE. What's the point? Strike while the iron is hot!

He goes up the stairs.

Scene Eight

GEORGE. Down you come! (*He comes down, followed by* YVONNE, LEO *and* MICHAEL.) Surprise, Surprise!

MICHAEL. All right, time's up. Right, is it animal, vegetable or mineral?

GEORGE. Michael, I'm afraid I'm going to have to tell you something that might hurt you.

MICHAEL. What do you mean hurt me?

GEORGE. Well my boy, it seems she has been weak. And I have helped her to be strong. She's told me everything. Apparently . . . there is someone else.

MICHAEL. Yes but Madeleine regrets that more than anybody – and it'll all be sorted out by tomorrow. Isn't that right, Madeleine?

GEORGE. I'll speak for her if that's all right. I promised her I would. The man you are referring to, she's quite prepared to give him up. Which leaves the other man.

MICHAEL. What other man?

GEORGE. You thought there were just two of you. When in fact there are three.

MICHAEL. And who's the third?

GEORGE. Michael, be a man. You're young, very young. You know nothing of women. You know nothing of life. This girl is in love . . .

MICHAEL. Yes, with me!

GEORGE. With you, indeed, I don't question the fact. But she is in the thrall, if you like, of a boy of her own age. And from her own social background. Who's there, behind the scenes, who has called your love into question. She was hoping to escape him by marrying you.

MICHAEL. But that's a lie, an invention. I know Madeleine. Maddy, speak to me. Tell them it's not true. Tell them it's a lie.

Silence.

But I know every tiniest detail of Madeleine's life. You're just a bloody liar.

YVONNE. Michael!

MICHAEL. Maddy, my love. Help me, save me. Tell me they're lying. Get rid of them!

GEORGE. Of course, this is a blow, and your reaction's perfectly understandable. But my dear boy didn't you ever think how little you saw of her – her evenings, for example, were very much her own . . .

MICHAEL. But who? Who? How? Where?

GEORGE. She was hoping for a miracle. She'd tried everything. But this man had her in his grip and wouldn't let go. She was his slave and did his bidding, whatever it was.

MICHAEL. If this is true – I'll kill her. (*He rushes to her.*) You tell me, or I'll . . .

YVONNE. Michael, what's come over you? You wouldn't hit a woman!

MICHAEL. I would. I'll slap her cheating face – that's all she deserves. (*He suddenly falls to his knees.*) Madeleine, little angel, I'm sorry. I know they're all lying, they just want to put me to the test, to see if I really love you . . . Speak to me. Speak to me. Have you forgotten our night together. *Today?* You! You! How dare you! Marry me as a trick, as a device!

GEORGE. That isn't quite what I said. She was hoping to free herself from his influence. I also said she loves you, but is in thrall to him.

MICHAEL. Well, now I see the whole disgusting story. And I was about to walk straight in to it. I'm going mad.

(*To* MADELEINE.) Who is it? Who is it?

GEORGE. She said that you don't know who it is. That you couldn't possibly know who it is.

MICHAEL. A heartless old bitch, you were right, Mama . . . absolutely right . . . and to think I almost insulted you.

YVONNE. There, there. Parents know best, my love. You've still got your poor old mother; there there . . .

MICHAEL (*freeing himself*). One last time, Madeleine. Talk to me, tell me. It's all a joke isn't it, a ghastly joke.

YVONNE. Calm down.

MICHAEL. Calm down she says. Up there, I was as jumpy as a cat. I was thinking, Papa's falling for Madeleine, he'll talk Sophie round, Leo's already on our side, it'll all be fine. And what do I find? A nightmare, a nightmare out of the blue, and all my dreams shattered . . . and a hundred nameless gibbering horrors . . .

MADELEINE (*hardly any voice*). Michael.

MICHAEL. And now she deigns to speak to me.

YVONNE. Michael, don't be unkind. She didn't have to admit anything, she could *easily* have got round your father and carried on as before, insinuated her way into our household, and exposed you to God knows what public scandal and disgrace. (*To* MADELEINE.) So in that respect, mademoiselle, we're grateful.

My dear, if there's *anything* we can do . . .

MADELEINE. I can't stand it! I can't stand it any more!

She runs up the stairs, disappears.

MICHAEL (*running after her*). Madeleine, Madeleine, Madeleine!

GEORGE. Leave her.

MICHAEL. I want to go home! Take me away from here.

No, I'm staying. I want to know everything.

GEORGE. Why?

MICHAEL. No, you're right, Papa. I don't want to know anything. I just want to go home. I want my room . . .

YVONNE. You'll be safe in there. And I'll come and rock you to sleep.

MICHAEL. I should never have left the gypsies.

YVONNE. You had to learn the hard way.

MICHAEL. Tidy here, isn't it. Lots of lovely order. But I suppose it's necessary, isn't it, so there's no chance of getting the visitors mixed up. Easier to spot a forgotten umbrella – a discarded shirt or a tie or an incriminating cigarette butt. Very much the modern style!

MADELEINE *appears at the top of the stairs. Pale.*

MADELEINE. Go now.

MICHAEL. Oh, it must be time for number three. We've got a rota system here. No stay. Relax, she'll be free in a couple of hours. But no of course she really loves him . . . and me . . . and the other one. Her heart's such a capacious organ, there's room for everyone inside.

YVONNE. Michael.

MADELEINE *collapses on the staircase.*

MICHAEL. Stay where you are Leo, leave her. It's more play-acting. The damsel swoons dead away.

YVONNE. She needn't have told us anything.

GEORGE *slips out.*

Scene Nine

MICHAEL. I've been sinking deeper and deeper into a cess-pit. Thank God Papa was there to haul me out. Sophie, Papa, how lovely to be loved simply and honestly, without double-dealing and deceit . . . I've had enough. Come on you gypsies, back to camp. So Auntie, Mama – where's Papa got to?

LEO. He hates scenes – he's slipped off home.

MICHAEL. He prefers his inventions to us. More reliable.

YVONNE. You're trembling.

MICHAEL. Not at all.

YVONNE. Yes you are. Come on darling, take my arm. We'll totter down together like a couple of old invalids.

Leo! We can't leave her alone in this state.

LEO. You see to Michael. Get him home. I'll stay with her a minute.

YVONNE. Thank you Leo.

Exit.

Scene Ten

LEO. Mademoiselle.

MADELEINE. Michael, Michael. Where's Michael?

LEO. There there, I'm still here. Calm down. Nice and calm.

MADELEINE. Oh madame, madame! Oh madame. Madame . . . madame . . .

LEO. There there, just relax.

MADELEINE. Madame, madame, you've no idea what I've . . .

LEO. I have. I think I've guessed.

MADELEINE. What?

LEO. That the other man and Michael's father are actually one and the same.

MADELEINE. How did you know?

LEO. Well, not to spot that you'd have to be blind, as blind as my sister and Michael. It was horrendous. But obvious. But the third man is a complete fiction. He doesn't exist?

MADELEINE. No, of course he doesn't. But Michael didn't doubt his existence for a second.

LEO. George bullied you into it, am I right?

MADELEINE. He tortured me. He threatened me. He wanted to 'cure' Michael, he said.

LEO. There are limits.

MADELEINE. Thank you, madame; thank you . . . I didn't think . . . I'd never have hoped . . .

LEO. That's all right. I've rather fallen for you. I didn't, to be frank, have that much confidence in George's choice of women, or Michael's, come to that. If this place had turned out to be another gypsy camp you might have won Yvonne's heart, but you certainly wouldn't have won mine. I didn't come here to be your friend, still less your accomplice. But now I see that I should like to be both. I think we should join forces against them – let's call it order versus disorder.

MADELEINE. But madame, what good would it be? Michael won't believe a word I say and George'll just start spreading lies again. It's pointless. It's finished..

LEO. Nothing is finished when it's based on falsehood. And that wasn't a real row, because those weren't real lies, so perhaps no real damage was done.

MADELEINE. I'm sorry, madame, I don't understand. Perhaps I don't belong to your milieu after all.

LEO. Milieu? Ha! it's hardly worthy of the name. Now listen, Madeleine, listen.

MADELEINE. I can't, I won't, I'm dead.

LEO. Don't you want me to bring you back to life?

MADELEINE. No-one can ever do that.

LEO. Will you please listen . . . Madeleine. Tomorrow, at five o'clock, you're coming to the gypsy camp.

MADELEINE. The gypsy . . .

LEO. To see us. And George.

MADELEINE. What, me?

LEO. Yes, you.

MADELEINE. They'll throw me out.

LEO. They won't, I'll make sure of that. Madeleine, there are times when I take revenge on other people's love because it disgusts me – and there are other times when love touches me to the very core of my being. So I'm a paradox.

How can we know what murky things go on inside us Madeleine? Don't try and understand me. Don't look too deep; God alone knows what lurks in the rag and bone shop of the heart. All right, I'm strange, I know.

MADELEINE. George made me swear . . .

LEO. He was merely taking revenge. Tomorrow he'll be a model father protecting his little boy.

MADELEINE. *Unbelievable.* Madame . . . how can I . . . express my gratitude.

LEO. Oh no, anything but that, not gratitude please. Any random action we take could randomly assist somebody else. It's all a mystery. So please, not gratitude – it's seldom appropriate . . .

MADELEINE. You have a kind heart.

LEO. No, I have a heart, but then everyone has a heart. I just hate disorder, that's all. I hate mess. And the mess made here today, by George, offends me. A horrid heap of dirty linen; it'll all need washing and ironing and tidying away. As usual. Come tomorrow.

MADELEINE. But . . .

LEO. No buts. And five o'clock. That's an order. Swear you'll come. On Michael.

MADELEINE. On Michael.

LEO. 'I . . . '

MADELEINE. . . . swear.

LEO. 'On Michael.'

MADELEINE. On Michael.

LEO. Splendid. Now get some sleep. Be ravishing tomorrow. Don't get your pretty eyes too red. My card.

MADELEINE. This nightmare.

LEO. It's already ancient history. I can find my own way out.

MADELEINE. And madame . . .

LEO. Ah – ah . . . what did I tell you, Madeleine – about gratitude?

Curtain.

ACT THREE

Scene One

Same decor as Act One. Starts dark, gets lighter as if the eyes were growing accustomed to the darkness.

LEO (*to* GEORGE, *who's just entered*). Still the same?

GEORGE. Still the same. I can't possibly stay in my room.

LEO. Well, I can't stay in my room. It's too ghastly. I've locked the connecting door, but that doesn't stop me hearing him moaning.

GEORGE. Michael's in a very bad way, but I'm not in that much better shape myself.

LEO. George, I refuse to equate your personal pain with this boy's misery. For a start he has no experience of the agony of love – and then, out of the blue . . .

GEORGE. He's got Yvonne.

LEO. Oh, for God's sake, George.

GEORGE. He's got Yvonne. He doesn't say a word but he holds her tight, tight, tight. And Yvonne's . . . triumphant. She's reunited with her son, with the prodigal. 'Reunited', that's all she keeps saying. *But what about me?* . . . When I told her . . . everything, when I emptied my heart, forcing it all out, her reaction was . . . 'Oh really? Well, fancy'. Hardly batted an eyelid. All she could think about was the potential danger to Michael, 'what if he knew?', how careful we had to be. All I got was this vague look in to the middle distance and, 'Well, that's your punishment, isn't it? . . . serves you right'.

LEO. Well, I don't think she's that far off the mark.

GEORGE. Christ almighty, not you as well? Punishment? Punishment, for what, for Christ's sake?

LEO. George, I stayed with the girl after you'd gone. Just the two of us. We talked – as much as she could in her condition.

GEORGE. Yes? And?

LEO. George, what you did was unforgivable.

GEORGE. What do you mean, what I did? What *you* did Leo, it was all your plan, you told me precisely what to do and what to say, in meticulous detail. It was your story, *your* invention.

LEO. I warn you; never ever let me hear you say that to anyone. Never ever repeat what you just said to a living soul, nor anything even vaguely resembling it. Is that clear?

GEORGE. Oh this is *un*believable.

LEO. Not the family cliché again. And, of course, yes, I heard her say it. But I heard all sort of things I hadn't heard before. And saw all sorts of things – and it was all quite different from what I'd heard and seen here. I was deceived, I was wrong, and I admit it. I misjudged you, I thought she might be some scheming little shop-girl, twisting you both round her little finger. And I was wrong. I'm sorry.

GEORGE. I see Madeleine's fooled you too.

LEO. No, no, no – she hasn't fooled me. She wouldn't know how. She's a child, an unhappy child.

GEORGE. Some child! She's grown-up enough to deceive me with my own son, not to mention . . .

LEO. Who? The third man? You're beginning to believe your own lies.

GEORGE. *Our* lies! No, yours, not mine.

LEO. George!

GEORGE. All right, all right . . . my lies. But who knows, we may well have stumbled on the truth . . . I mean a girl like that . . .

LEO. George – you are not going to believe this blasphemy to serve your own ends.

GEORGE. So we're canonising her now, are we? The blessed Saint Madeleine! The Virgin Maddy!

LEO. George, you're not listening. The point is that I have done something wrong and that that wrong has to be put right . . .

GEORGE. Aha!

LEO. Oh, for Christ's sake . . . you see, I don't know what I'm saying any more, that *you've* done something wrong which has to be put right, at all costs . . . All right then, that *we've* done something wrong. The important thing is that we have to undo it without Yvonne being any the wiser.

GEORGE. You mean go back on yesterday? You must be joking! Never in a million years.

LEO. Make a sacrifice. It's good to make sacrifices.

GEORGE. You're starting to sound like Yvonne.

LEO. I have to make you understand and you have to make

Yvonne understand. You have to pay for this, and so must she.

GEORGE. And what about you? This is outrageous. You set yourself up as judge and jury over the whole world. (*Noticing her disapprobation.*) What are you going to sacrifice? What have you ever sacrificed?

LEO. A lot, long long ago.

GEORGE. What do you mean?

LEO. How do you know you haven't already had my sacrifice, and now I'm calling in my debt.

GEORGE. Oh yes, what sacrifice is that? I'm dying to know.

LEO. You. I was in love with you, George. Who knows, perhaps I still am. I sacrificed myself to assure your happiness. But I was wrong. I don't intend to be wrong again. It's quite unthinkable that you should sacrifice Michael and that poor girl just to make life a little more convenient, a little less embarrassing, for you.

GEORGE. Leo.

LEO. No, not that – no affection, no gratitude . . . I can do without all that. No, this has to be done, George, we have to talk Yvonne round.

GEORGE. And me?

LEO. You know what has to be done.

GEORGE. You mean bring Madeleine here?

LEO. What else?

GEORGE. Even if I, for a minute, agreed to the torture of having those two billing and cooing anywhere near me . . . even then, Yvonne would go mad. She'd refuse, point blank, scream the place down, the works. She's been 'reunited' with her little boy, her little Mickey. And that's all she wants to know.

LEO. All she's got is a husk, a shadow of him. She'll work that one out soon enough.

GEORGE. She'd rather hold his corpse than see her son in someone else's arms.

LEO. That's monstrous. I know, we're all flawed, but this goes beyond common decency.

GEORGE. What would we say to Michael?

LEO. We'll say that Madeleine's been extraordinary (which isn't far from the truth), that she invented the third man to set Michael free, to return him to the bosom of his family, his rightful milieu. She didn't feel worthy of him. You see?

GEORGE. I never knew that you were so . . . big-hearted.

LEO. Big or small, my heart never gets used; it's nice to use it now. I love Michael. How could I not. He's your son.

GEORGE. And do you love Yvonne, Leo?

LEO. Don't dig too deep in anyone's heart, George; not in yours, not in mine. There's all sorts of stuff in there. Sometimes it's better not to know. George, this family is a wreck, a hopeless, hypocritical, middleclass mess, hanging on desperately to its false values as it rolls inexorably to its inevitable doom, like some dreadful juggernaut, crushing everything in its path – hopes, dreams, possibilities, everything. But we can salvage something before it's all too late.

GEORGE (*Lowering his head.*) Leo, I think you're right.

Silence.

LEO (*kindly, as if addressing a good little boy*). George . . . I do love you.

Scene Two

YVONNE *enters, same costume as in Act One, dishevelled.*

GEORGE. Darling, we were waiting for you.

YVONNE. It's intolerable.

LEO. Did he say anything?

YVONNE. No. He held my hand so tight I thought he'd crush it. I tried to stroke his hair but he wouldn't let me. I asked him if he was thirsty – he said, 'go away'. I hovered by the door. I was hoping he'd call me back, tell me not to go . . . And he just said, 'go away'. I can't bear it. *I can't bear it.*

GEORGE. I'll go . . .

YVONNE. If he doesn't want me that means he doesn't want anybody. I begged him to at least lie on the bed and he started pounding the floor with his fists. He's just lying face down in the dark.

LEO. Did he close the shutters?

YVONNE. Shutters, curtains . . . he's rolling from side to side, chewing at his shirtsleeves. He can't bear it, he's in agony, poor Mickey. If that girl weren't such a slut, I'd call her – I'd give her to him. That's how low I've sunk.

LEO. That's easy to say . . .

YVONNE. No, Leo – it's not easy to say. The fact I *can* say it shows what a state I'm in.

LEO. You want to give her to him..? That's what you want..?

YVONNE. Yes, whatever . . . I really can't bear it anymore.

LEO. To be honest, Yvonne, that's just what I wanted to hear you say. And I didn't want to say it first, or to have to make George say it. So, George, please, yes I think George has something to say.

YVONNE. Oh God, here we go again, more words.

GEORGE Yvonne, where we are now is the result of a crime – and I'm the perpetrator of that crime.

YVONNE. You?

GEORGE. Yes Yvonne. Madeleine is completely innocent. The mysterious third man doesn't exist.

YVONNE. I don't understand.

GEORGE. Leo, you tell her.

LEO. When I stayed with her yesterday . . .

YVONNE. You're such an innocent, Leo. She's tricked you into thinking that George is the culprit. He's the victim!

GEORGE. It's all right, Leo, I'll do it. Yes Yvonne – I've played a shameful part in all this. I forced that girl to lie, to sully herself. I invented the whole thing. I knew Michael was credulous enough to swallow it whole, and that Madeleine would be too terrified to contradict me.

YVONNE. You did that?

GEORGE. Yes, I swear I did.

YVONNE. George! You bloody fool, you could've *killed* Michael!

GEORGE. *And* I could've killed Madeleine as well by just turning up like that. So having plunged her into a state of catatonic shock, I took advantage of the private chat, which you'd insisted we have, to administer the *coup de grâce* and finish her off completely. Nice work. My best invention ever. The only one of my inventions which has actually worked. I was even quite proud of it. Until Leo came along and rubbed my nose in my own mess.

LEO. George . . . George, it wasn't just you, without me . . .

GEORGE. Without you, I'd've just let it carry on. And that's that. I want to take responsibility for all this and take it on my own.

This whole gypsy existence has its own irresistible charm, and that charm comes from Yvonne, but it makes us deaf and blind to the real world.

YVONNE. George, you're being ridiculous. You think you're touching greatness now. What in God's name are you dreaming of? What's done is done, and yes it's been vile. But neither Michael nor this woman have died. They're going through a crisis, that's all, like you are, like we all are, for God's sake. All we should do is to thank our lucky stars that none of it was anywhere near as bad as we'd feared and to make the most of our good fortune.

LEO. But Yvonne, what do you mean by good fortune?

YVONNE. Well, I suppose it was fortunate that the old chap turned out to be George.

GEORGE. Oh, thanks a lot.

YVONNE. Because if it had been someone else, George, I know you, you wouldn't have the guts to do what you did.

GEORGE. Guts? What I did was vile and inexcusable and motivated only by revenge. And my shoddy excuse is that I was doing it for you; merely obeying orders . . .

LEO. My dear George, my dear Yvonne, you're just not getting through to each other, are you?

GEORGE. Well what's she saying?

LEO. Yvonne, if I've got this right, is saying it's fortunate, in spite of the damage that's been done, that Michael thinks he can't possibly marry her.

YVONNE. But . . .

LEO. Whereas George is trying to say that henceforward he won't stand in their way.

YVONNE. In whose way?

GEORGE. Michael and Madeleine's, they're in love.

YVONNE. What are you saying?

GEORGE. I'm saying that we nearly killed those children, and out of pure selfishness, and that it's still not too late to bring them back to life. That's what I'm saying.

YVONNE. Are you really seriously suggesting, I mean quite calmly and objectively suggesting, that that woman could ever assume our name – or belong in our class?

GEORGE. Your grandfather collected semicolons, hers was a bookbinder, I mean, you've already something in common . . .

YVONNE. I'm not joking, I'm asking you seriously.

GEORGE. How can I give a serious answer to a ludicrous question. Our name, our class? You make us sound like something from the Almanac de Gotha. Listen, I'm a second rate inventor – a mediocrity, a failure. You're a semi-permanent invalid who sits around in darkened rooms. And Leo's an old maid who's stayed an old maid to help us out. And that's it! That's us! And it's for *that*, for all this emptiness and mess and disappointment that you wish Michael to turn his back on . . . real possibilities and fresh air and open space. No, no, I won't allow it.

LEO. Bravo, George.

YVONNE. Yes, bravo George, he's a God now, he's infallible.

LEO. I just admire him, that's all.

YVONNE. That's not all . . . You love him, *that's* all!

GEORGE. Yvonne!

YVONNE. You two get married then . . . . have a double wedding. I'll just disappear. I'm obviously in the way – I'll just leave you all to it – it's easily done.

LEO. You're falling apart.

YVONNE. Yes, Leo, I am, and can you blame me?

LEO. No, I can't.

YVONNE. Thank you. I'm sorry.

LEO. Don't thank me, and don't say sorry. I'm not interested. Listen Yvonne, listen to this. If I'd really wanted George I wouldn't have let you take him. I would have found a way.

YVONNE. Pah!

LEO. But it's too late to dredge it all up now. There's only one way of repairing some of our damage, and that's by stopping it happening to Mickey. By bringing him back to life.

GEORGE. We've got to help him Yvonne . . . now.

YVONNE. But, in any case, she's miles too young.

GEORGE. Yesterday you were saying she's too old . . .

YVONNE. No she's too young . . . compared to me.

GEORGE. That's grotesque . . .

YVONNE. You're asking the impossible.

GEORGE. We asked the impossible of Madeleine – and she did it.

LEO. Don't fight yourself, Yvonne . . .

YVONNE. I've been reunited with my boy, I'm not going to lose him again.

GEORGE. The Michael you've found is in purgatory, he's a ghost, he scarcely exists.

YVONNE. It's too much, it's too much.

GEORGE. Yvonne. Force yourself, tear yourself open, show us your heart.

YVONNE (*breaks away*). Leave me alone. What right have you to take a moral tone with me? You're no nobler than I am. It's all lies – filthy filthy lies. Very well, lie yourselves out of this one.

(*To* GEORGE.) Yesterday, when we arrived at that woman's flat, I remember this perfectly, you pretended you weren't sure whether we were on the right floor or not, you pretended not to know her flat. Both of you, in league . . . you dared to take me to see your mistress.

GEORGE. Be quiet!

YVONNE. Your kept whore!

GEORGE. Shut up – are you mad? What if the boy were to hear you?

YVONNE. I'd explain.

GEORGE. You'd get it all wrong and make it all worse. You're a complete mess, all hopeless mess and confusion.

YVONNE. But that's how we live. Both of us.

GEORGE. Yvonne, there are moments, God knows few enough, when we are able to undo the damage we've done, and save ourselves by saving others. Yvonne, darling, do it, do it for me. Join us.

YVONNE. What, summon Michael? See that woman? Humiliate ourselves?

GEORGE. Stop this pompous nonsense. We're not 'summoning' anyone. All we have to do is to go to Michael, to hold him in our arms, tell him the good news, and change his whole life.

LEO. And I can vouch for Madeleine.

YVONNE. Leo, what have you been up to, what have you done?

LEO. No more than my duty. I talked to her, listened to her, comforted her. And telephoned her.

YVONNE. You telephoned her?

LEO. Yes, I asked her to come here.

Exits.

Scene Three

YVONNE. Is this what you've been plotting?

GEORGE. Leo did it off her own bat – but I'm grateful to her.

YVONNE. You're going to force me, aren't you?

GEORGE. We're going to save you, save ourselves. And save Michael.

YVONNE. She's wormed her way into all your hearts.

GEORGE. Don't talk like that. It's no good.

YVONNE. Leave me alone, I need time. I can't stand all this.

GEORGE. You think this has been easy for me.

YVONNE. Poor old you.

GEORGE. And poor old you. Not that we're that old, Yvonne, either of us . . .

YVONNE. One day we notice that the children have grown up and want to take our place.

GEORGE. I suppose that's the natural order of things.

YVONNE. I wouldn't know – order's not my forte.

GEORGE. Nor mine . . . you're freezing.

YVONNE. Oh. Am I?

LEO *re-enters.*

Scene Four

LEO. Let's get things ready for our little party. I 've lit the candles on the tree. That'll be nice and festive.

GEORGE. I'm not very good at parties, or surprises.

YVONNE. But when you spring them, they certainly are spectacular!

LEO. Children, please, no quarrelling!

GEORGE. What are you planning to do?

LEO. Very simple. Yvonne, you've got to tell him, he's got to think it all comes from you.

YVONNE. But . . .

LEO. No buts.

YVONNE. I don't want to do this . . .

LEO. I know, and above all don't let her see that . . .

YVONNE. I'll look completely phony. And I'm freezing here. Look. Listen. My teeth are chattering.

GEORGE. It's nerves.

YVONNE. One day I'll drop down dead and you'll say, it's nerves. My knees are knocking together.

LEO. Here, lean on me. But you must do it.

GEORGE. You must, Yvonne.

Door slams.

LEO. A door slam. It's Michael. You see, a miracle . . .

YVONNE. What are you doing to me?

GEORGE (*listening*). What's he doing? Where's he off to?

LEO. If he's going out . . .

YVONNE. . . . then he'll slam the other door.

LEO. That's right.

YVONNE. He hasn't eaten since yesterday. He's in the kitchen. He's hesitating. He's coming to my door. He's listening, he's reaching out for the door knob. Turning it . . . .

The door knob turns.

He's opening the door. (*The door opens slowly.*) I'm frightened, that it mightn't be him – that it might be something . . . horrible . . . Leo, George. What's wrong with me. Mickey!!!

Scene Five

MICHAEL. Sophie, it's me.

YVONNE. Come on, come in. Shut the door and come in.

MICHAEL. All right, I'm shutting it. I'm not staying. I just came to get some sugar.

YVONNE. You know where it is.

MICHAEL. Yes. Are you all alone?

YVONNE. My poor baby – can't you see, there's your Auntie, and your Papa.

MICHAEL. Oh, sorry Leo, sorry Papa. I can't see very much. Am I in the way?

He goes in to the bathroom, returns eating sugar.

GEORGE. Not at all, your mother was just about to go and find you.

MICHAEL. Also . . . I wanted to . . . I had to speak to you Mama, and since what I have to say to you, I also have to say to Papa and to Leo, its good that you're all here together. First, Sophie, I'm so sorry I sent you away, and I'm so sorry I was rude to you. I couldn't bear it . . . you understand . . .

YVONNE. I understand absolutely. My poor Mickey.

MICHAEL. I don't want to be pitied.

GEORGE. So what did you want to tell us?

MICHAEL. This. Obviously I can't spend the rest of my life flat on my tummy on the floor of my room. So, Papa, that job, the one you said was mine if I wanted it, in Morocco . . . well . . .

YVONNE. You're going to leave me!

MICHAEL. I've made my mind up.

YVONNE. Mickey!

MICHAEL. Oh, Sophie . . . I wouldn't be much fun if I stayed here – and besides I'll only infect you all, and drive you all insane.

YVONNE. You're mad!

MICHAEL. I would be if I stayed here. I can't stay here. I can't stay in this house. It's impossible. So since I have to go . . . I'd rather it was somewhere a long way away. And I'll work. I'm just a dabbler, and a wastrel . . . I am. And the thought of suicide disgusts me. So I have to find some space, some fresh air . . . to see new things . . . And Europe, you know . . . (*He makes a 'forget it' gesture.*)

YVONNE. But what about me? What about us?

MICHAEL. Oh Sophie!

YVONNE. Give me your hand. Now listen, Mickey. How would it be if you didn't have to go?

GEORGE. If, for example, we were to tell you some wonderful news.

MICHAEL. There's no such thing any more – not for me.

LEO. Say if the reasons for your wanting to run away, I mean move on, say they were to disappear?

YVONNE. Say your motives for leaving Europe and for leaving us were to just vanish into air. How would you feel then?

MICHAEL. That's enough, Sophie. I'm going back to my room. And papa . . .

GEORGE. No Michael, you are not to go back to your room. I *do* have wonderful news for you – amazing news. Madeleine . . .

MICHAEL. Don't even mention that name again . . . I forbid anyone to ever speak of her again. Never. Never *ever*. Just don't touch me . . . there . . . please. It's all raw and bleeding. Just shut up, the lot of you.

LEO. Michael! Listen to your father.

MICHAEL. I won't! I will not have her name mentioned. Just leave me alone, will you. Why are you still torturing me?

GEORGE (*stopping him going*). I'm sorry. I know it's painful but we have to talk to you and we have to talk to you about her.

MICHAEL (*defeated*). What do you want with me?

GEORGE. Your aunt stayed behind yesterday, after we'd left.

MICHAEL. You're off again . . . you're trying to get me to stay here by inventing lies. You're wasting your time.

YVONNE (*a cry*). You mustn't leave us!

MICHAEL. You see!

GEORGE. No, you mustn't leave us . . . it would be *criminal* to leave us.

MICHAEL. What d'you mean?

GEORGE. Criminal, because even if your own family counts for nothing any more, there is still one person who deserves better, who deserves that you should at least ask her permission to go.

MICHAEL (*laughing horribly*). Oh I see – of course. Silly me. She . . . was very clever with you, (*That is* GEORGE.) and she even managed to charm her way around Leo.

LEO. It's not that easy to lie to me, believe me.

MICHAEL. I don't believe anything anymore.

GEORGE. That would be a big mistake . . . Yvonne.

YVONNE. Please believe him, Mickey.

GEORGE. You know your mother wouldn't lie.

MICHAEL. You're torturing me.

GEORGE. All we're saying is that this girl is not only completely blameless, but also completely wonderful. She thought she wasn't up to our class, our milieu. So she lied. The whole story was a complete and utter fiction. She invented it on the spot – for *you*. To set you free, so we could be rid of her.

MICHAEL. But that's awful. I believed her!

GEORGE You believe bad as readily as good.

MICHAEL. Tell me, mama, tell me.

YVONNE. I've already told you.

MICHAEL. Then we must find her. She might have run away, or . . . Where is she, where is she?

LEO (*her door*). She's right here.

YVONNE. Here?

LEO. Yes, she's been hiding in my room since five o'clock this afternoon.

MICHAEL *faints away.*

Scene Six

YVONNE. Mickey, Mickey. He's ill!

GEORGE. Look Michael, it's Madeleine. She's come to see you.

LEO. Madeleine, you help him. Speak to him.

MADELEINE. Michael, Michael. Yes, it's me. Are you all right?

MICHAEL. I can't believe it, I just passed out. How ridiculous. Maddy, my love, my love. (*He holds her* – YVONNE *moves away.*) I don't know what I'm doing fainting! I should be running and shouting and jumping for joy!

MADELEINE. Just kiss me, you silly thing.

MICHAEL. Forgive me Madeleine, do forgive me, say you'll forgive me! Please, please, forgive me.

MADELEINE. Why should I forgive *you* – after all the pain I've caused you.

MICHAEL. I've been so stupid and such a pig. (*They kiss.*) Are you cold?

MADELEINE. I was suddenly freezing, just now, when you'd fainted – I'm better now – I couldn't see a thing when I came in.

GEORGE. You couldn't see anything because no-one can – this is the Stygian gloom Michael's mother seems to favour . . . and if you suggest turning the lights on you get your head bitten off . . . (*He notices* YVONNE's *absence.*)

LEO (*to* MICHAEL, *aside*). Michael, your mama . . .

MICHAEL. Where is she?

MADELEINE. It'll be to do with me.

GEORGE. Nonsense – she was here and quite happy a moment ago.

LEO (*to* MICHAEL). You ought to go to her and give her a kiss.

MICHAEL. I thought she was still here. (*Calling out.*) Sophie!

YVONNE (*from the bathroom*). It's all right, I haven't got lost. I'm in here. Just doing my jabs.

MADELEINE (*loud*). Do you need any help, Madame?

YVONNE (*loud*). No thanks. I'd much rather be on my own.

LEO. She hates being helped. She's obsessive about it.

They're whispering now.

MADELEINE. I might be able to talk her out of it one day.

MICHAEL. That'd be quite an achievement.

LEO (*to* MADELEINE). I warn you, Yvonne's hypersensitive. Of course you're besotted with each other – which is entirely as it should be, but children, take care, eh?

MADELEINE. That's what I meant. I was worried I'd offended her or something.

GEORGE. Not at all. And Leo, stop portraying Yvonne as some sort of were-wolf.

LEO. I'm not, I'm just warning them. We mustn't make Yvonne jealous.

GEORGE. That's right, scare her off!

MICHAEL. Stop it Papa. Madeleine's intelligent enough to know what's what . . .

MADELEINE. I'm not scared – but I am a little anxious . . .

GEORGE. Well then, perhaps you *should* be a little careful . . .

The door from the bathroom opens. YVONNE, *looking unsteady. Her voice is odd.*

YVONNE. You see, mademoiselle, how much they all love me. I'm away for a tiny second and they're completely lost without me. I wasn't lost. I was just sorting myself out.

She goes to the bed and collapses on it.

Mademoiselle, I'm an old old lady. I'd be dead without my insulin.

LEO. Michael give her a kiss.

MICHAEL (*trying to take* MADELEINE *along too*). Come on!

MADELEINE. No, you.

GEORGE (*to* YVONNE). Are you all right?

YVONNE (*with effort*). I'm f . . . . . . .ine.

MICHAEL *leaves* MADELEINE *and goes to the bed.*

MICHAEL. Sophie, are you a happy bear?

YVONNE. Very happy. (MICHAEL *tries to kiss her.*) Don't push me around! Mademoiselle, you be careful, he's like a hopeless puppy, he'll be kissing your ears and tugging at your hair!

LEO (*clapping her hands to distract them*). Michael, shouldn't you show Madeleine your famous room?

MADELEINE. Michael, you'll surely allow me to see your room?

MICHAEL. You'll only start cleaning it up!

MADELEINE. I wouldn't dare!

GEORGE. I'll go too. I'll show you my gun, if you're interested.

MICHAEL. The grand tour of the camp. Step this way . . . Sophie, we'll leave you with order personified.

YVONNE. Mickey! Stop! Stay where you are!

GEORGE. What is it. Yvonne! Yvonne!

YVONNE. I'm scared . . .

MICHAEL. Not of us?

YVONNE. I'm so scared. So dreadfully scared. Stay here! Stay here! George! Mickey! Mickey! I'm so terribly scared!

LEO. It's not the insulin. She must have taken something else.

GEORGE. What have you done?

YVONNE. My head's spinning, George. I've done something stupid. Something really really stupid. I . . .

MICHAEL. What? Tell us, Sophie!

YVONNE. I can't. I wanted to . . . Help me! Save me Mickey. I saw you all together, when I was in the corner. And I thought that I was in the way, just an encumberance.

MICHAEL. Mama.

GEORGE. God help us!

YVONNE. I lost my nerve. I wanted to die. But now I don't want to die. Now I want to live. I want to live with you. And see you . . . happy. Madeleine, I'm sure I'll grow to love you. I promise I will. Hurry. Do something. Save me. I want to live. I'm so frightened. Help me!

MADELEINE. Do something someone! For God's sake.

GEORGE. Michael, stay calm. Get the doctor, upstairs. Get him down, force him if you have to – I'll telephone the clinic.

MADELEINE (*to* MICHAEL). Michael, come on, hurry up.

She shakes him. He rushes out. We hear a door slam. The whole of the rest of the act should be punctuated by door-slams.

GEORGE. You could go mad in this house.

Exit.

Scene Seven

MADELEINE. Her pulse is very weak. It's regular – but very weak.

LEO. I knew something was wrong. I knew it . . .

MADELEINE. It's my fault. I don't belong here. I should leave.

LEO. Leave?

MADELEINE. Leave Michael, madame.

LEO. Don't be stupid. You stay here. Anyway, Michael will need you. Just as George will need me.

YVONNE. I can hear you Leo.

LEO. What can you hear?

YVONNE. I heard you. You forgot that I could hear you.

LEO. Hear what?

YVONNE. You act the innocent. You just want to be rid of me . . .

LEO. Yvonne!

YVONNE. I poisoned myself. And now I'm going to poison you.
I'll poison you all. I saw you, when I was in my corner, I saw
you, saw the lot of you. You wanted to chuck me on the scrap-
heap. That's what you wanted – that's what you all wanted.
Mickey! Mickey!

LEO (*shouts*). Georgy!

Scene Eight

GEORGE (*entering*). Her specialist is out of town, they're sending
someone else . . .

LEO. George, Yvonne's becoming delirious.

YVONNE. I am not delirious. They want to drive me away, to
boot me out, to get rid of me. I saw what was going on. And
now I'm going to tell. Absolutely everything.

GEORGE (*kissing her on the lips*). Calm down . . . calm down.

YVONNE. It's been years since you kissed me on the mouth. And
now you're only doing it to shut me up.

GEORGE (*stroking her, but trying to shut her up*). There there.
Don't excite yourself, nice and quiet!

YVONNE. I will, I'll poison you too. I'll tell. I'll tell Mickey . . .

MICHAEL (*rushing in*). No-one's there. No-one's answering . . .

YVONNE. Michael, listen to me . . . listen to me, Michael. I don't
want you to . . . I don't want you to.. I want . . . I want you to
know . . .

LEO (*overlapping the foregoing – drowning YVONNE out*).
Michael, your mother's delirious. Go and give the clinic
another ring. Madeleine my love, please, go and help him. He
can't manage on his own. Come on, quick as you can.

She pushes them out while YVONNE *says* . . . .

YVONNE. Stay here. Stay here. I order you, Mickey. Mickey, it's a trick. They're trying to get you out of the room. It's a ruse. You bastards! I'm not going to let you get away with this filthy business.

LEO (*terrifying*). Yvonne!

YVONNE. And you, you engineered the whole thing! You wanted me dead so you could have George to yourself.

GEORGE. That's grotesque.

YVONNE. It is . . . quite grotesque . . .

She falls back into bed.

GEORGE. Where's the doctor? If Michael took a cab . . .

LEO. They'd pass each other on the way.

GEORGE. But what shall we do? What shall we do?

LEO. Wait, just wait,

YVONNE (*opening her eyes*). Mickey – are you there? Where are you?

GEORGE. He's here . . . he's coming back.

YVONNE (*sweetly*). I promise I won't be bad . . . I wouldn't . . . It's just that I saw everything . . . from over there . . . and I was alone, all alone in the world. You'd forgotten me. I only wanted to be helpful. I feel giddy, George, help me up . . . Thank you . . . Leo, is that you? And that girl . . . I know I'm going to like her. I want to live. I want to live with you. I want Mickey to be . . .

LEO. He'll be happy, and you'll see him happy. Now lie down. The doctor's coming. We'll look after you.

YVONNE (*a relapse*). What? It's you. Still you. You and George. Arrest them, somebody. I want to give evidence. I'll tell the whole truth. Ah! Ah look. They're shit scared. Don't you touch me – don't come anywhere near me. Police, get the police. Let them come. Help. Michael! Michael! Help. Michael! Michael! Michael! Michael! Michael! Michael! Michael! (*She's screaming.*) Michael! Michael! Michael! Michael! Michael! Mickey! Mickey! Mickey! Mickey! Mickey! Mickey! . . .

She is still.

GEORGE and LEO (*during the foregoing*). Yvonne, please, I beg you. Lie down, Keep calm. You'll exhaust yourself. Listen to me – please – help us . . .

GEORGE. She can't be.

He buries his face in the bedcovers.

Scene Nine

MICHAEL (*enters with* MADELEINE). It's impossible. No answer. I'll go myself.

LEO. There's no point.

MICHAEL. What the hell'd you mean?

LEO. Michael, Michael, your mother is dead.

MICHAEL. What?

GEORGE Mickey, my poor Mickey.

MICHAEL. Sophie . . .

LEO *moves away from them. She addresses* GEORGE *and* MADELEINE.

LEO. Look at you all. You'd give anything to bring her back to life . . . So you can keep on torturing her . . .

MICHAEL (*moves to* LEO). Leo!

GEORGE. Michael, you're forgetting your mother.

MICHAEL (*stamping his foot*). Sophie's not my mother, she's my best friend. Tell them Mama, you've told me a thousand times. Tell them . . .

MADELEINE (*horrified*). Michael, you're mad!

MICHAEL. Christ, I forgot. I'll always forget.

He breaks down, by the bed.

I'll never understand . . . . Never.

A ring in the hall. LEO *exits.* MADELEINE *rests her head against* MICHAEL's.

MADELEINE. Michael, Michael – my love, my love.

The bell rings.

LEO (*returning*). It was just the cleaner. I told her that there was nothing for her to do . . . that everything was in order . . .

Curtain.